# WALLS OF WATER

# WALLS OF WATER

## A REVELATION OF GOD IN THE MIDST OF DELIVERANCE AND BEYOND

### KEVIN F. WINKLER

Walls of Water

A Revelation Of God In The Midst Of Deliverance And Beyond

Kevin F. Winkler — Woodway, Texas

Walls of Water © 2024 — Kevin F. Winkler

All rights reserved.

Unless otherwise noted, Scripture quotations are taken from the Amplified® Bible, Classic Edition (AMPC). Copyright © 1954, 1958, 1962, 1964, 1965, 1987 by The Lockman Foundation. Used by permission. All rights reserved.

Scripture quotations marked NKJV are taken from the New King James Version®. Copyright © 1982 by Thomas Nelson. Used by permission. All rights reserved.

Scripture quotations are from the Revised Standard Version of the Bible, copyright © 1946, 1952, and 1971 by the Division of Christian Education of the National Council of the Churches of Christ in the United States of America. Used by permission. All rights reserved.

Scripture quotations taken from The Holy Bible, New International Version®, NIV®. Copyright © 1973, 1978, 1984, 2011 by Biblica, Inc. Used with permission. All rights reserved worldwide.

Scripture quotations marked (NLT) are taken from the Holy Bible, New Living Translation, copyright ©1996, 2004, 2015 by Tyndale House Foundation. Used by permission of Tyndale House Publishers, Carol Stream, Illinois 60188. All rights reserved.

Published by: Winkler Writing Enterprises www.winklerwritingenerprise.com

Cover design: Rachel Howarton - pastor@thechurchalive.com

For inquiries or permissions, contact:

kwinkler@thechurchalive.com

ISBN: 979-8-9926539-0-8

Library of Congress LCCN: 202590374

Printed in the United States of America.

# CONTENTS

# ACKNOWLEDGMENTS

I want to thank several people for their help and support. No one is an island to themselves. This book was truly a team effort and a testimony that anything is possible with the right people around you!

First and foremost, I'd like to thank Jesus for the permission and the encouragement to write.

Your words to me in the fall of 2022 helped to propel this project. You said: "Write your books and plan your events," and here we are. Thank You, Lord, for Your help and Your faithfulness to me. I love you so much. I look forward to however much time I have left on the earth to continue to serve You, and I look forward to being with You forever in eternity.

Next, I'd like to thank my lovely bride, Misty. Behind every great man is a wonderful woman, and don't know where I'd be without you. Apart from Christ, you are the most important person to me. I love you. Thank you for cheering this book onward.

I could not move on to anyone else yet without acknowledging my not-so-little one. I am glad the Lord blessed us with a person just like you who loves the Lord and loves to write, too. You spur me on, and I look forward to writing together.

A special thank you to my mother, whose seeds of faith and love for the Lord were planted in me from the very beginning. There is no one who could have ever taken your place. I love you. Thank you for the gift of life and for introducing me to Jesus. To my mother-in-law, thank you for catching the fire and vision for Church Alive before anyone else did. You planted the first financial seed to build this ministry, and it will never be forgotten.

Thank you also to Pastor Alex and Rachel Howarton and the

Church Alive family. Thank you to Ivy, who began the process of transformation on this book. I appreciate the first review. However, I am honored and grateful for Kelani Daniels, who took this book, and through the work of the Holy Spirit and her gifts, developed this into something even greater. Father, thank You for helping us to rely on other people created in your image, and not to try to do it alone. This was indeed a group effort.

And Jesus, thank You for the unknown person You sent to reiterate Your instructions on this endeavor. Her name was Whitney, and that's all I know. But she had a Word from the Lord to get to it and not stress about it, and I feel I have done my best to honor this.

# FOREWORD

"But whatever were gains to me I now consider loss for the sake of Christ. What is more, I consider everything a loss because of the surpassing worth of knowing Christ Jesus my Lord, for whose sake I have lost all things. I consider them garbage, that I may gain Christ and be found in him, not having a righteousness of my own that comes from the law, but that which is through faith in Christ—the righteousness that comes from God on the basis of faith. I want to know Christ—yes, to know the power of his resurrection and participation in his sufferings, becoming like him in his death." (Philippians 3:7-10 NIV).

In these four verses one can genuinely sense the passion, the zeal, and the relentless hunger of the devoted apostle Paul to pursue the Lord Jesus Christ with his entire being. He was willing to trade his "everything" that he might gain Christ. Even after knowing Him in an intimate, personal, way, Paul still pressed forward "to know Christ" in every possible way that was yet beyond his own experience---including "the power of His resurrection and participation in His sufferings, becoming like him in His death."

Paul encouraged us to do likewise. He said, "Be imitators of me, as I am of Christ" (1 Corinthians 11:1 RSV). I know someone who does just that; who has become an imitator of Paul's zealousness as he was of Christ. In the more than twenty years that I have known Pastor Kevin Winkler, I have seen in him an example of one who pursues the Lord Jesus Christ in like manner as Paul did, willing to lose everything for the sake of gaining Christ. Kevin is untiring in his pursuit to know his Lord in a greater and more intimate degree than the day before.

Even as Pastor Winkler writes about embracing the "walls of water" moments in our lives that we might encounter God through personal revelation, he is writing about the true passion of his own life. He is genuine. He is…just as he speaks (or, in this case, as he writes).

Kevin encourages us not to settle for second-hand revelations of God in our lives, but to settle for nothing less than a first-hand seeing for ourselves the face of God, and thus he speaks of his own heart-cry. He exhorts us to leave the grandstands and engage ourselves in the game, not as spectators, but as participants in the grandest purpose of all times.

I pray that you will catch the vision to see the Lord for yourselves as Pastor Winkler leads you to a deeper understanding of the eternal beauty and the life-building experiences of your very own "walls of water" moments.

May the Lord bless you as you ever seek to make Jesus Christ preeminent in all aspects of your life. Amen.

John J. Howarton - Missionary

# INTRODUCTION

"So, the people of Israel walked through the middle of the sea on dry ground, with walls of water on each side!" (Exodus 14:22 NLT)

Can you imagine what it was like for these people—men, women, youth, and children—to walk through a canyon made of walls of water? I can imagine the Israelites walking through and people looking over and seeing fish swim by, like in an aquarium. Perhaps a young child reached over and touched the water, with a parent nervously exclaiming, "Nobody touch nothin'!"

This jaw-dropping journey of God's people through the Red Sea reveals to us that there is a God who is able to make a way in a situation where there seems to be no way.

Like them, I've had my share of moments when God stepped into a situation to deliver me just in time. In many of these situations, there would have simply been no way out, no solution to the problem, apart from God stepping in and making a way. These were what I refer to as "walls of water" moments. Just as God made walls of water out of the Red Sea so the Israelites could cross over, He has stepped into difficult and even impossible situations in my life and brought deliverance.

In these moments, not only did I get relief and solutions to the situations I found myself in, I also gathered "jewels"-deeper understanding about what God is like and revelation He wanted to show me through the trial I was facing.

I'm sure you can relate to moments like these. You find yourself in an impossible situation, and just when you think you're gonna fall through, God steps in.

This is why I believe, with all my heart, that the Lord has called me to write. His exact words to me were, "Write your books and plan your events."

My experience with the Lord in these moments, along with the truths in Scripture, are what have shaped the content of this book. Just as the Bible declares that everything written in former days is for our instruction and hope (Romans 15:4), our life experiences can also be beneficial and uplifting to others. Through this book, I pray you will see how God continues to meet us in our own "walls of water" moments.

During those times of struggle—when we feel cornered by life's troubles and long for deliverance—God's love, patience, and care become clearer than ever. This book is designed to highlight these divine rescues and deliverances in our lives-these moments where God personally opens a way for us-whether through an actual miracle or a perfectly timed word that settles our hearts.

By remembering these rescues, you and I can rekindle hope, fight discouragement, and press on in faith. The benefit? A deeper aware-ness of God's faithfulness, renewed strength to face obstacles, and the encouragement to keep running the race He set before us.

Yet, there's more to these stories than meets the eye. Sometimes, the situation itself has a purpose we only understand once we're on the other side of the trial. Why does it seem like God waits until the last possible moment to intervene? Why does He allow us to face "impossi-ble" circumstances?

As we explore these questions, we discover that God wants to reveal facets of Himself we could never have known otherwise—just like the Israelites who encountered Him in a whole new way while crossing the sea on dry ground.

In these pages, I'll reference several stories and Scriptures. Reading them firsthand will help you fully absorb what God wants to show you. Throughout this book, we'll look back on people who walked through miraculous events, reflect on modern parallels, and learn how to "let the redeemed of the Lord say so" by rehearsing our own miracles again and again.

Most of the time, we only see the big picture in hindsight, when our 20/20 vision kicks in. But if we give God plenty of room to work and keep believing, we can experience breakthroughs that send our hearts soaring. I pray that these insights, stories, and Scriptural truths spark an unshakable hope in you. The Lord is eager to pour out personal experiences of deliverance to remind us He's always working, even when it seems all is lost.

With this in mind, I invite you to journey forward. Let's remember what God has already done for us, stay in the good fight of faith, and keep our eyes open for the walls of water God may be parting in our lives today.

Blessings!

Kevin Winkler
Sr. Pastor, Church Alive

# CHAPTER 1
# CHEESEBURGER REVELATIONS

---

[THAT YOU MAY REALLY COME] to know [practically, through experience for yourselves] the love of Christ, which far surpasses mere knowledge [without experience]; that you may be filled [through all your being] unto all the fullness of God [may have the richest measure of the divine Presence, and become a body wholly filled and flooded with God Himself]! (Ephesians 3:19)

Imagine for a moment that someone is telling you about the juiciest bacon double cheeseburger they've ever tasted. The bun was buttered and toasted, the meat seared to perfection with melted cheese, and the veggies were crisp and fresh. They claim it was the best cheeseburger they've ever had.

You can picture it in your mind and enjoy the secondhand experience as they share their satisfaction with you. But to actually hold one in your hand, or better yet, take a bite of the best cheeseburger ever for yourself—wow! Your taste buds know that there's a difference between secondhand knowledge and firsthand experience.

In the same way, God wants us to have more than a secondhand experience with Him. Hearing about what He has done through messages, teachings, and testimonies is good. But as followers of Christ, we need more than to just hear stories—we need deeper experiences with God; encounters that impart revelation knowledge to us that helps us know Him better.

## Why Revelation Matters

Revelation:

1. The act of revealing or disclosing; disclosure.
2. Something revealed or disclosed, especially a striking disclosure, as of something not before realized.[1]

Each of us needs to hear about the Lord's mercy, kindness, and wonder. But even more than this, we need to *personally experience* these things so we can truly know Him.

Personal revelation—God's revelation of Himself and His ways—is of utmost importance. We learn about Him through His Word, through our prayer time, through visions and dreams, and by Him directly manifesting His help in our lives. When we do so, we move from simply memorizing the Scriptures to living them out!

Jesus even alluded to revelation knowledge as He was working with His disciples. At one point, they were traveling by boat and realized they had forgotten to bring bread. Jesus then told them to "take heed and beware of the leaven of the Pharisees and the Sadducees." (Matthew 16:6) Jesus was not talking about bread at this moment, although this is what they thought. He was actually cautioning them against the doctrinal error of the Pharisees and Sadducees and teaching them that a little error can permeate their whole belief system.

Jesus pointed out the importance of truly perceiving beyond "physical bread" (head knowledge)—He was illustrating how revelation knowledge from the Father is what changes us.

He alluded to revelation knowledge again later in this chapter. He asked His disciples who people were saying He was, and they listed off names.

"Some say John the Baptist, some Elijah, and others Jeremiah or one of the prophets." He said to them, "But who do you say that I am?"

Simon Peter answered and said, "You are the Christ, the Son of the living God." Jesus answered and said to him, "Blessed are you, Simon Bar-Jonah, for flesh and blood has not revealed this to you, but My Father who is in heaven." (Matthew 16:14-17, NKJV)

Clearly, there is knowledge deeper than what we understand on the surface. This is revelation knowledge, and God desires to share this with us. However, it is our responsibility to position ourselves both to seek Him and to be open to what He's trying to show us, especially in the midst of difficult situations.

And He said to them, "Be careful what you are hearing. The measure [of thought and study] you give [to the truth you hear] will be the measure [of virtue and knowledge] that comes back to you—and more [besides] will be given to you who hear." (Mark 4:24)

. . .

**Parables: Revealing Truth to the Receptive**

If God has truths He wants humans to understand, you would think He would just come straight out and tell us, right? Unfortunately, that's not how it works. Instead, Jesus used parables to teach about the kingdom of God.

Parable:

1. A short allegorical story designed to illustrate or teach some truth, religious principle, or moral lesson.
2. A statement or comment that conveys a meaning indirectly by the use of comparison, analogy, or the like.[2]

Why did He do this? He was checking to see if people had ears to hear what the Spirit was saying. The Spirit, or the Holy Spirit, is the Spirit of truth. In Mark 4:34, the Bible states that Jesus didn't tell the people anything without using a parable, "but privately to His disciples (those who were peculiarly His own) He explained everything [fully]."

He also gave a more full explanation in Matthew 13:10-17 about why He spoke in parables.

Then the disciples came to Him and said, "Why do You speak to them in parables?"

And He replied to them, "To you it has been given to know the secrets *and* mysteries of the kingdom of heaven, but to them it has not been given. For whoever has [spiritual knowledge], to him will more be given *and* he will be furnished richly so that he will have abundance; but from him who has not, even what he has will be taken away. This is the reason that I speak to them in parables: because having the power of seeing, they do not see; and having the power of hearing, they do not hear, nor do they grasp *and* understand. In them indeed is the process of fulfillment of the prophecy of Isaiah, which says: You shall indeed hear *and* hear but never grasp *and* understand; and you shall indeed look *and* look but never see *and* perceive. For this nation's heart has grown gross (fat and dull), and their ears heavy *and* difficult of hearing, and their eyes they have tightly closed, lest they see *and* perceive with their eyes, and hear *and* comprehend the sense with their ears, and grasp *and* understand with their heart, and turn *and* I should heal them.

But blessed (happy, fortunate, and to be envied) are your eyes because they do see, and your ears because they do hear. Truly I tell you, many prophets and righteous men [men who were upright and in right standing with God] yearned to see what you see, and did not see it, and to hear what you hear, and did not hear it."

When you consider these verses in light of Matthew 16:13-20, where Jesus asked His disciples who people were saying that He was, we see that *true* understanding, which is seeing Jesus as the Christ, the Son of the living God, came through revelation from the Father, not from human knowledge about God.

This is confirmed by Jesus' response to Peter's confession. When Peter said, "You are the Christ," Jesus emphasized that no human had revealed that knowledge to him, but that it had come by revelation from the Father. Such divine knowledge is also available to us today and is precisely the sort of personal revelation that transforms our lives.

## The Church Built on Revelation

In Matthew 16:18, Jesus said, "And I also say to you that you are Peter, and on this rock, I will build My church." Could God be revealing, through this verse, that He would build His church on the rock of revelation knowledge?

Everything in the church hangs on the fact that Jesus is our savior and Messiah. The Lord will not let the church be extinguished. He will not let the gates of hell prevail against it. Over the centuries, many people, nations, and organizations have tried to put the church out of the way. But God will not allow it. Nothing will ultimately win against her.

He has given the church great power on the earth. We have the authority to bind and loose, and He's given us the keys of the kingdom of heaven—just as he said in Matthew 7:7: "Ask, and you will be given what you ask for. Seek, and you will find. Knock, and the door will be opened."

When Jesus asked the disciples who they said He was, and when Peter rightly declared who He was, it was not a moment where Jesus was "lifting Peter up." It was about shining light on the revelation that Jesus is, indeed, the Christ.

We need revelation knowledge. We need divine light to shine clearly on our understanding—it makes all the difference in the world.

We are accustomed to relying on our physical senses and assessing our world through what we take in. God gave us our senses so we could experience His creation. However, it's different when it comes to understanding God. Peter was only able to grasp who Jesus truly was through revelation knowledge, which was beyond what his senses could understand. This was something only God could give.

God desires to be known. He's not hiding Himself on purpose. He wants us to truly know Him, and not just at a distance through the limits of human speculation. But the way to truly know God accurately is through revelation, not merely head knowledge.

## How God Reveals Himself Today

God has never stopped making himself known to His people; what happened in biblical times still happens today. If revelation, which has the ability to transform our lives and our perspectives, is so important, how do we get it? What do we need to do to position ourselves to truly know Him?

1. **Scripture.** We must immerse ourselves in God's Word. The Holy Spirit illuminates the written Word, bringing passages to life and revealing God's heart, character, and plan.
2. **Prayer and devotion.** As we spend time alone with God and bring our petitions to Him, we sense His guidance, conviction, and comfort, which in themselves can serve as revelation. He can also say things to us that enlighten our understanding.
3. **Visions and dreams.** Just as in biblical accounts, God can use supernatural means to communicate messages uniquely tailored to individuals.
4. **Holy Spirit's promptings.** The Spirit can nudge us toward certain actions, give us peace or caution, and confirm truth in our hearts as we listen.
5. **Community and counsel.** Sometimes God speaks through trusted believers or mentors who can share a word of wisdom or insight that resonates with our spirit.
6. **In the midst of trials.** When we face difficult situations, if we seek God for help, we are actually in a prime position to receive revelation of some aspect of God's character and nature. These are the "walls of water" moments that have the ability to deeply impact both our understanding of God and our personal relationship with Him and others.

When we encounter God through personal revelation, it's transformative because it reshapes our relationship with Him from being theoretical to being intimately real. We see His kindness, wisdom, and power in ways that textbook knowledge can't convey. Faith becomes personal conviction. Hope becomes a living expectation. Instead of only believing what we hear about God, we experience Him for ourselves, and that changes everything. As Paul said in Ephesians 3:10-12,

[For my determined purpose is] that I may know Him [that I may progressively become more deeply and intimately acquainted with Him, perceiving and recognizing and understanding the wonders of His Person more strongly and more clearly], and that I may in that same way come to know the power outflowing from His resurrection [which it exerts over believers], and that I may so share His sufferings as to be continually transformed [in spirit into His likeness even] to His death, [in the hope], That if possible I may attain to the [spiritual and moral] resurrection [that lifts me] out from among the dead [even while in the body]. Not that I have now attained [this ideal], or have already been made perfect, but I press on to lay hold of (grasp) *and* make my own, that for which Christ Jesus (the Messiah) has laid hold of me *and* made me His own.

Likewise, in John 17:3, Jesus clearly defined what eternal life means, and it is to truly know God.

And this is eternal life: [it means] to know (to perceive, recognize, become acquainted with, and understand) You, the only true *and* real God, and [likewise] to know Him, Jesus [as the] Christ (the Anointed One, the Messiah), Whom You have sent.

*Walls of Water* is about discovering more intimately who God is through the process of deliverance, rescue, and physical and spiritual intervention. It's about seeing Him in a way we could not know without revelation, which is life-changing.

## Prayer

Father, In Jesus' Name: I love You. I need You. Thank You for revealing Yourself. God, if You did not disclose who You are to me, I would not know You. Thank You that Your Word says that eternal life is to know You. I want to become more deeply and internally acquainted with You, my God. In Jesus' name, amen.

# CHAPTER 2
# FROM THE GRANDSTAND

---

THEREFORE THEN, since we are surrounded by so great a cloud of witnesses [who have borne testimony to the Truth], let us strip off *and* throw aside every encumbrance (unnecessary weight) and that sin which so readily (deftly and cleverly) clings to *and* entangles us, and let us run with patient endurance *and* steady *and* active persistence the appointed course of the race that is set before us,

Looking away [from all that will distract] to Jesus, Who is the Leader *and* the Source of our faith [giving the first incentive for our belief] and is also its Finisher [bringing it to maturity and perfection]. He, for the joy [of obtaining the prize] that was set before Him, endured the cross, despising *and* ignoring the shame, and is now seated at the right hand of the throne of God. (Hebrews 12:1-2)

When you truly know and trust Jesus, who is merciful, kind, and benevolent, you cease to constantly question His decisions. You no longer need to understand why He acts as He does, because you possess revelation knowledge about His character that has deepened your trust. He is good, all the time! This revelation grants us profound peace and joy.

As already emphasized, God wants us to know Him. He desires more than mere human understanding of Himself—He seeks personal comprehension of His being. He wants our relationship with Him to grow in love and trust, and this is nearly impossible to have apart from revelation knowledge.

Through revelation, God causes us to know things we wouldn't be able to know otherwise. Because He knows us so well as our Creator, He understands the things we specifically need to understand to help us overcome.

God yearns to reveal Himself to us in tangible ways, not merely as an observer in the grandstands of life, but as one engaged in the game alongside us. Moreover, as we mature, He stands as a coach on the sidelines, encouraging us when we find ourselves deep in life's struggles. Then, because He has helped us, He equips us to do the same for others.

Looking at how God revealed Himself to people in the Bible gives us hope for our own journeys. You may be familiar with the story of Job. He is a man who walked blamelessly before the Lord and pleased God. The devil appeared to Him and God asked him in Job 1:8,

"Have you considered my servant Job, that there is none like him on the earth, a blameless and upright man, one who fears God and shuns evil?"

Satan argued that the reason this was the case was because God had "blessed the work of his hands, and his possessions [had] increased in the land" (v. 10). This is an intriguing exchange behind the veil of the unseen world and offers insight into Satan's nature and tactics. What's most interesting to note here is God's assessment of Job. He declares that Job is "blameless" and "upright." Can you imagine God saying that about you? What God says about us, not what the world says about us, should be the paramount concern for us all.

We can be the most degreed person on the earth and possess numerous earthly accolades yet be wicked in God's eyes. We can be one of the wealthiest people on earth with the ability to buy whatever we want, gaining political clout and influential standing among men, but be filled with evil. Conversely, we may be seemingly insignificant in the eyes of man but have significant favor in the kingdom of God.

Can one be both rich by worldly standards and godly? Yes, Job exemplifies such a person. Nonetheless, many may struggle to balance both. That is why I believe that many kingdom people may not be financially well off on the earth (though I strongly believe that poverty is not God's way). I think there are enough Scriptures that deal with the issue of prosperity to show us that this is actually God's desire for us, as long as we do not idolize money or possessions.

Job wasn't destitute; God blessed and protected him, as evidenced in Scripture. Yet, God allowed Satan to test Job and gave him permission to wreak havoc in his life with the condition that he didn't destroy Job himself. It's important to note how God responded, affirming Job's righteousness and allowing the devil to test Job within certain bounds.

His story also supports the idea that nothing can touch us or enter our lives unless God allows it. Of course, this presupposes our obedience to the Lord and the absence of open spiritual doors due to sin, which grants the enemy legal access to our lives.

## Co-heirs With Christ

There is a common misconception regarding prosperity in the context of Job's story. Some individuals, misinterpreting God's desire for prosperity, accuse those who preach about it of promoting what is termed a "prosperity gospel." However, it's crucial to acknowledge that God's Word reveals His desire for prosperity in various forms, both spiritually and materially. Job's story illustrates this truth. Those who criticize this perspective often overlook the biblical principles underlying God's blessings and provision.

I've been accused of preaching a "prosperity gospel" from individuals who were not committed to serving the Lord. They criticized my emphasis on positivity and prosperity, unaware of the biblical foundations supporting these teachings.

The essence of the gospel is inherently positive. It's a transition from death to life, from being ostracized from God to becoming co-heirs with Christ in His kingdom, where even the streets are paved with gold. Isn't this the epitome of prosperity?

Satan indeed wreaked havoc in Job's life, destroying all of his flocks and his property, killing his children, and even inflicting boils upon Job himself—all in one day. As we reflect on Job's experiences, we are faced with the question of suffering and endurance. While we may express a desire to emulate Job's steadfastness, few would willingly endure such trials.

Job's wife's encouraged him to curse God and die, and three of his friends told Job that he must have committed some sin for this to happen to him. Yet despite his wife's discouragement and the misguided counsel of his friends, Job persevered in his faith. His friends' attempts to console him only led to further accusations and misunderstandings.

Throughout this ordeal, Job maintained his innocence and expressed his desire for answers from God. His willingness to question and seek understanding reveals the depth of his faith and his commitment to truth and encourages us to do likewise.

## Our Spiritual Struggle

Many years ago, my wife and I found ourselves in an immense spiritual struggle. It came seemingly out of the blue and shocked us to the core.

We reached out to our friends and family to ask for prayer. In the midst of the difficulty, I could sense the Lord assuring me of his protection, but along came our adversary to accuse and concoct crazy scenarios of what was happening. We can see a bit of this "reasoning and theories" over in 2 Corinthians 10:4-5:

For the weapons of our warfare are not physical [weapons of flesh and blood], but they are mighty before God for the overthrow *and* destruction of strongholds, [Inasmuch as we] refute arguments *and* theories *and* reasonings and every proud *and* lofty thing that sets itself up against the [true] knowledge of God; and we lead every thought *and* purpose away captive into the obedience of Christ (the Messiah, the Anointed One).

The enemy indeed is a master deceiver and manipulator. Without the Lord's help, we are no match for him. If the Lord were not to have given us power over the enemy, how would we have prevailed?

The sheer absurdity of the mental reasonings, theories, and lofty ideas that spiritual forces were speaking to us was like being blasted with arrows from all sides. The enemy prowls around like a roaring lion looking for someone to devour. He does this in the form of outright lies and half-truths in an attempt to put people into bondage. This bondage comes in the form of mental strongholds. The enemy lies and tries to deceive us to block God's will in our lives and make us miserable.

As stated before, I knew in my heart, and so did my wife, that God was going to keep us safe and rescue us. But our minds were bombarded with lies that told us the contrary. We vacillated in our faith; we were strong in one moment and then had times of doubt. Would this be like this forever? Would we overcome? Would the sun shine again over our lives?

Have you ever felt like this during a trial? The middle of a trial can feel like a dark place that has no exit. After a period of time that seemed to last forever, God stepped in. He gave me a vision while I was in the shower one morning, as a relentless round of lies and deceit assailed my being.

He showed me a picture of Noah's Ark floating high above the mountains. The rain had already ceased, the sun was already shining on the world, and the water was still like glass. There was no wind and no movement. God spoke a word firmly and forcefully into my mind and heart during that vision, saying, "Quiet!"

In an instant, the trial and trouble was over. That moment in the shower was a "walls of water" event for my wife and me.

He does not always explain His paths in our lives. But I know He will be faithful to you as He was to me. That revelation of God's power and care deeply blessed us and is still blessing us today. And one last thing here: you cannot deliver yourself. Only God can deliver you. He possesses the wisdom and insight you need to get free.

I'm sure Job was mentally bombarded with reasons, theories, and lofty ideas that the devil presented to him about what was happening in his life. Then, in Job 38:1-4, something incredible happened: God spoke.

Then the Lord answered Job out of the whirlwind and said, "Who is this that darkens counsel by words without knowledge? Gird up now your loins like a man, and I will demand of you, and you declare to Me. Where were you when I laid the foundation of the earth? Declare to Me, if you have *and* know understanding."

Before the Lord spoke, there was no indication that anything would be different about that day than from the many days of suffering that had preceded it. I believe Job might have felt the same way-like he had already endured a lifetime of suffering that would never end.

## Job's Encounter with God

God spoke to Job, and his friends also heard it. This was a pretty spectacular thing in itself. We know that God speaks to us. And He speaks through different ways, but in this instance, I believe God definitely spoke in an audible voice. At this moment, all of Job's trials and troubles came to a sudden halt. As the Lord began to question Job, the only thing Job was probably seeing was God's mighty hand in the midst of his situation.

I believe that God had always planned to rescue Job in the end. He has His own reasons for why He did what He did, and as far as we know, He never actually told Job the purpose for all the suffering he had to endure. The reality is, when it comes to faith, we will sometimes have unanswered questions.

The rest of Job's story centered around the Lord speaking about what He had made, how things operated, and asking Job questions about creation that Job couldn't answer. This moment was the turning point of all of Job's suffering.

God stepped in and granted a measure of revelation. Without this, Job would have concluded that God had abandoned him. As the Lord spoke from the whirlwind, it was as if Job had stepped off the land down into the Red Sea. God "parted the waters" with him through dialogue. This was a "walls of water" moment for Job, and he even mentioned that things God had shared were too wonderful for him to even know! I believe Job saw God in a whole different light as a result of this experience.

In the deliverance, in being brought out of suffering, can we see God in a way that is clearer and more majestic? The One who allows us to go in is the One who never leaves us. He is here to lift us up and save us. Do we want to be lifted up, though? Are we willing to see God in a new light?

Out of all the stories of people written within the Bible, other than Jesus Himself, I think probably Job suffered the most (or at least it seems that way). Even the disciples, who were all martyred for their faith, may not have suffered as much as Job.

I don't think any of us would ever want to actually go through what some of these people experienced. We might talk a big talk, but when it comes down to where the rubber meets the road, would we really want to be crucified upside down like Peter, or have our head chopped off like John the Baptist?

If we had to die for our faith in Jesus, that would be God's will. We all need to be ready to give our lives if necessary. But that does not mean we run right out and try to get killed. God rescued many people from actual premature death, just as God spared Job's life. He did not allow Satan to kill him.

I believe when Job came up out of the "water" after the experience with God in the whirlwind, he was able to serve God in a way that was deeper, more meaningful, and more faith-filled than he had before. Then, God blessed and protected Job, restoring to him more than what he had lost. This demonstrates God's willingness to grant prosperity and safeguard His faithful servants. I believe Job came up and out of the walls of water as a new man, with renewed trust in the One who is more than able.

I hope you and I will do the same.

### Prayer

Father, thank You for protecting us from the evil one. Thank You for Your hand on my life. Please help me to live for You all the days of my life, giving You honor in private and in public. Please forgive me of all my sins and help me to live by faith in Jesus' name.

# CHAPTER 3
# THE IMPOSSIBLE

———————

AND HE SAID TO THEM, Be careful what you are hearing. The measure [of thought and study] you give [to the truth you hear] will be the measure [of virtue and knowledge] that comes back to you—and more [besides] will be given to you *who hear*. (Mark 4:24)

God wants to show out in mighty ways. He loves to thwart the enemy's plans and rescue His kids through His mighty power in situations that seem like they have no way out.

Not every deliverance is as big as the parting of a sea. But when *you* are the one being plucked out of a situation—oh, it's big deal alright. During these times, I believe for you, for me, and for others, it is God showing out because He can. He is the Almighty, and there is none like Him.

God used Moses to lead His people out of Egypt, where they had been in bondage for hundreds of years since the time of Joseph. A new pharaoh had risen who was not kind to Joseph, as the first one had been, and he became cruel to the Israelites. They cried out to God, and He raised up Moses to deliver them.

Pharaoh would not allow the Israelites to leave his land, but through a series of ten plagues, God demonstrated that He was more powerful than any god the Egyptians worshipped. He led them out of Egypt, and the Egyptians pursued them to the Red Sea. This was where their "walls of water" moment happened: God parted the Red Sea and led the entire nation successfully across. When the Egyptians tried to cross, the waters caved in and killed them all.

*It would be good to take a minute to read about Moses right up to the crossing of the Red Sea. This is found in Exodus 1:1-14:31.*

You would think the Israelites would be so grateful that their awe of God would carry them right into the promised land. Yet this is not the nature of humans. They did not carry the revelation they received during their deliverance—that God would step in and help them when they needed it. Instead, when God brought the Israelites to the border of this precious possession He wanted to give them. The spies they sent over to scout the land out came back and showed the Hebrews the produce of the land. And how wonderful it was, BUT the spies said there were powerful people living there. The people heard how big these people were. They began to doubt and complain. They did not hang on to the revelation they received during the parting of the Red Sea. They doubted God could help them in this situation. The same situation God brought them to. Ten spies scared the people and said it could not be done—taking the land. But only two spies said God was fully able to give it to them—lets go take the land! The Israelites believed the ten and did not want to go in...

So, because they failed to believe. Because they grumbled about God. God was displeased with them, and a journey that should have only taken approximately eleven days ended up taking forty years. Wow! What a turn of events.

Fast forward forty years after the Israelites crossed the Red Sea, they found themselves on the side of the Jordan River opposite Jericho. Back at the same place they failed before. The Lord again parted the waters for them to cross (Joshua 4:13). Can you imagine the sight of this before this new generation of Israelites? As soon as the priest carrying the ark stepped down from the bank into the water and stood in the Jordan River, it started to pile up.

When God steps into our situations, it's so big in our eyes. Sometimes, we're even facing life and death moments where we get to see His mercy and protection in a way we haven't seen before. Then there are other times when we are simply struggling with satanic lies and God gives us some kind of reprieve, and often in ways we'd never expect.

**Small Bills**

This happened recently to me. I found myself facing what seemed to be a hopeless situation. But the truth is that with God, there are no hopeless situations.

One morning, I ran payroll for our organization. It's not a whole lot of money, but I must have it in order to pay the team, myself. I logged into the bank account to notice $19 was deposited from our online donation system. I had just prayed that God would cause there to be enough money in there when I looked.

Nervousness about what I would see in the account is nothing new to me. Over the years I have struggled as it relates to the ministry bills. There have been plenty of times Misty and I had to personally cover the lack of finances. Miraculously, God would always allow us to obtain it through other means.

This time I just prayed, logged in, and saw $19. My heart sank a bit. We had a larger offering several weeks before, and when this happens, I always try to save as much as possible in order to store up for times when we might need it… and we needed it. There was not enough to pay me, but just enough to pay the team.

Was God leaving us out in the cold? Couldn't He see that He had called us to this, and we had heeded His call? We "keep showing up." If we were trying to live for Him and stay away from sin, then why were we constantly struggling?

This time, however, I was determined not to let my heart be discouraged. I chose to stay positive and be thankful to the Lord for allowing us to serve him. Paul said in Philippians 4:11-12,

Not that I am implying that I was in any personal want, for I have learned how to be content (satisfied to the point where I am not disturbed or disquieted) in whatever state I am. I know how to be abased *and* live humbly in straitened circumstances, and I know also how to enjoy plenty *and* live in abundance. I have learned in any and all circumstances the secret of facing every situation, whether well-fed or going hungry, having a sufficiency *and* enough to spare or going without *and* being in want.

Instead of the same old, "Why Lord, why?" and "When, Lord, when?" I responded with, "God thank you for your help." He knows, and He sees. The Apostle Paul was also called to serve as a mouthpiece of God, so of all people, why did he also experience lack?

I decided, during this trial, that I was not going to continue the pattern of crying and complaining I had done previously! I was not going to allow the devil to tell me that there must be something wrong with me and my ministry, or that other people don't have to worry with ministry finances (yeah right—I know there are many).

I paid the team. I thanked the Lord. And about that time, I noticed a message on my Facebook Messenger app. I tapped on the icon and saw a message from someone I had served with at a church eighteen years prior.

Everyone knows and understands that as people move from one church family to another, although they tend to stay in contact, it doesn't always happen. They end up in a new church with a new focus. Of course there are exceptions, and we are always friends and family members of the great global church, which includes our previous pastors.

Even if we love the pastors we were under and those we served with, the reality is, pastors always have people coming and going. My wife and I understand this because people have come and have gone in our ministry as well. For many, it was not God's will for them to leave, and for many it was.

I read the Facebook message from our long-time friend, and it seemed like it came out of the blue. I responded to her, and when she responded back, she realized that instead of sending a Facebook Marketplace post of a nice car to her husband, who is also named Kevin, she sent it to me.

Was this a coincidence? I don't think it was. I believe in divine appointments, especially in times when God knows we need them. She took the time to explain the mix-up, but then she went a step further. She sent an encouraging message that was so spot on, you would have thought she had been in the heart of the conversations with the Lord and knew how I had been pushing through just moments before. But God did! He saw! He knows!

She said,

"Hey Kevin! Peace, brother. I was trying to send this to my husband Kevin and picked you instead. I will take this opportunity to speak joy, peace and hope to you. You have poured out into so many lives and at times you don't see the fruit. But it will be there! All God's promises are yes and amen. Stand on those and not what your human eyes can currently see!"

To some, this may not seem like a big deal. But I knew what had been going on in my heart. I know the conversation I just had moments before, and for years prior! I know the Holy Spirit quickens people to send us words and messages when He is trying to speak to us. I reached out and thanked her and let her know that the timing of her message was perfect. And the car was nice too!

Perhaps it seems like a small thing. After all, we did not need thousands of dollars—just a few hundred to meet that week's payroll. To God, our response to tests and trials is a big deal. We can do the "right" thing in the physical realm but have a negative heart attitude toward it. But when we can do the right thing and also have the right heart about it – that's a win for you and for the kingdom of God.

Our Father does not delay our promotion for no reason. He does not hold us back as a joke or withhold blessings to be mean. As a loving Father, I believe He uses everything and every situation in our lives to grow us for eternal life.

I believe my decision to be thankful this time and not mope around caused Him to say, "Well done, son. I know this has been a very, very long time of struggling and trying to maintain a good attitude, even when it did not look like there would be any physical fruit from it."

When we are walking through seemingly impossible situations and God steps in and reveals Himself, this is when we see Him so clearly. There's something about suffering that positions our hearts to be more receptive to what He has to reveal to us.

He is so good, and I would not have traded these years of waiting for anything. If I had known how long this was going to take, how many tears and frustrations I would have had, I still would want to do this again. The only thing I would have done differently was to enjoy the process more.

Did my story end with a rainbow over a pot of gold? No. But was payroll met? Yes! The resource came in. And the Lord caused my personal bills to be covered once again. Yet for me, the true wealth came in the form of the breakthroughs that happened in my heart. It's always about our faith and His Word. God can make what we do have to stretch further and cover more, and He did.

It's in these times when God is opening a way that is absolutely impossible to us that we experience the depth of His love and His help at a deeper level. He is giving us revelation in the midst of trials; "walls of water" that reveal what He's like in a more impactful way.

What are some of the areas, places, and circumstances you have lived through that you can see as a "walls of water" event? Has there been a situation in your life that if God would not have stepped in and delivered you, there could have been a major problem? When God did step in, did it radically change you and your understanding because you could see Him more clearly in the midst of it?

When I was a kid, I grew up around the church. I had a young love for it and liked going. My mom was Southern Baptist and my dad was Missouri Lutheran. Other than sharing core Christian beliefs, these denominations could not have been more different.

I loved the Lord and felt like I was saved as a young child, but over my teenage years and into my early to mid-20s, I drifted away from Him. I would say that I was on a trajectory that was not in line with God's will at all. But God, through the use of discipline, brought me back to Him and I have never left Him since.

I pray that your understanding of Him grows. He is very active in our lives if we let Him be. He does hear us and He does see us. His heart wants to be not just towards a nation like the nation of Israel, but to individual people.

Examine your life. Spend time thinking about all He has brought you through. Give thanks, praise, and acknowledge Him.

**Reflective Exercise to Recognize Your Own Walls of Water**

Take a moment to think and pray about your own "walls of water" moments. Reflect on these questions:

1. Think of a time when circumstances seemed absolutely impossible, yet at the last minute, something changed. Who or what intervened, and how did that moment affect your view of God?
2. Consider a "small bills" scenario in your life—a relatively minor financial or practical need that God met in a clear and timely way. How did your faith respond before and after that provision?
3. Name a "Red Sea" or "Jordan" moment in your life. This would be a scenario that felt insurmountable and like it had no solution. Can you see, in hindsight, how God led you through?

Take a few minutes to write down these memories. Offer thanks and praise to God for each one. As you recall them, ask the Holy Spirit to show you any fresh insight or gratitude you might have neglected to give Him.

Share Your Story: We would love to hear your stories. Your testimony is unique to you and should be told. Feel free to reach out to us. Our contact information is at the end of this book.

## Prayer

Father, in the name of Jesus, I thank You for Your care and concern for me. Lord, if it was not for You, where would I be? What would have become of me? But You did step in and deliver me, and I thank You for it. Please help me to take time to rehearse what You have done in my life. I will continue loving You and sharing these things with others. I love You, my God. In Jesus' mighty name, amen.

# CHAPTER 4
# BULLETPROOF

---

THEN NEBUCHADNEZZAR the king [saw and] was astounded, and he jumped up and said to his counselors, Did we not cast three men bound into the midst of the fire? They answered, True, O king.

He answered, Behold, I see four men loose, walking in the midst of the fire, and they are not hurt! And the form of the fourth is like a son of the gods! (Daniel 3:24-25)

A life-changing incident happened to me when I was about fifteen years old. My brothers and I, along with some friends, were at my grandparents' farm. At that time, taking a few small-caliber rifles out to plink cans or bottles in the junk area was normal. We had grown up with guns in our lives, had been taught how to use them, and by this time, were quite capable of handling them safely.

We made our way down to the area where old bottles, cans, and other scrap were kept. Armed with our .22 rifles, we set up a few items for target practice. We had done this many times before without any issues, and this day was supposed to be no different. As we set up the bottles and began shooting, the bullets made contact with the glass, causing them to explode. It was fun, and we were having a good time.

## Bulletproof by God's Hand

At some point, I shot at one of the bottles about thirty yards away. If you've ever heard a bullet ricochet off something, there's a unique sound—a whistling *zrooooooommmmm*! On this particular shot, the bullet bounced back toward me, which was not the norm. The sound of it coming was loud and fast, and I instinctively knew it was on a path towards my head. Even though it wasn't a large bullet, any contact with a teenager's head would have been devastating.

As it whizzed through the air, I could hear it coming—*zzzzrooooooommmmm*! But then, a miracle happened! About two feet from my head, the sound changed to a *thud* as it hit the ground at my feet. I looked down and saw a bent piece of lead—the bullet!

It was almost as if a hand had reached into the physical realm and stopped the bullet in its tracks. It went from a thousand feet per second to zero. It was an extraordinary divine intervention-one that I can hardly believe even now.

At that time, my relationship with God wasn't what it is today, but this event is dear to me. It helps me see how the Lord can step in and even make me "bulletproof."

.   .   .

### Shadrach, Meshach, and Abednego: Fireproof by God's Hand

In Daniel 3, we see another story of incredible divine intervention in the lives of Shadrach, Meshach, and Abednego. Their story is intertwined with Daniel's—the same Daniel from the story of the lion's den. All these men were part of the group that got hauled off to Babylon because Israel wasn't obeying the Lord as they should have been.

At this point, Israel was living in a foreign land and serving a foreign king with customs and ideas much different from their own. The Lord gave these men favor with their captors, and because of Him, they received places of influence and leadership with the king.

As time went on, the king decided he needed a big ol' statue of himself ninety feet tall. He wanted everyone to bow and worship the statue. Well, the three young men couldn't do that. They were worshippers of the one true God, and He has a bit of a problem with people worshipping anyone or anything but Him.

The king heard that Shadrach, Meshach, and Abednego did not worship the statue, and he got his feathers ruffled about it. He decided to give them another chance to bow down and worship it, but they held to their convictions, knowing it would cost them.

In a rage, the king had the guards crank up the furnaces. He had them bound and thrown these men into the fire as punishment for their rebellion. But by the power of God, an absolutely amazing thing occurred.

Then Nebuchadnezzar the king [saw and] was astounded, and he jumped up and said to his counselors, Did we not cast three men bound into the midst of the fire? They answered, True, O king. He answered, Behold, I see four men loose, walking in the midst of the fire, and they are not hurt! And the form of the fourth is like a son of the gods! (Daniel 3:24-25)

. . .

Veggie Tales phrases it this way: "He was reeeeal shiny!" The Lord stepped in and made these people fireproof. This was a "walls of water" moment for them.

Can you imagine the thoughts that were racing through their minds right before being thrown into a raging fire? Or the flood of emotions they would have undoubtedly experienced, hearing the order to "Throw them in!" The next moment, they were in the presence of the Lord, who put His hand over them and shielded them from the power of the flames.

I can imagine the awe and the sheer joy they experienced in that moment! They saw God do the impossible. How could anybody go through this and not see our Lord in a new light?

By stepping in, God was doing more than just saving them-He was impacting an entire kingdom. Nebuchadnezzar, the most powerful man in the kingdom of the most powerful nation at that time, did not know the Lord nor His power.

Then Nebuchadnezzar came near to the mouth of the burning fiery furnace and said, "Shadrach, Meshach, and Abednego, you servants of the Most High God, come out and come here." Then Shadrach, Meshach, and Abednego came out from the midst of the fire.

And the satraps, the deputies, the governors, and the king's counselors gathered around together and saw these men—that the fire had no power upon their bodies, nor was the hair of their head singed; neither were their garments scorched *or* changed in color *or* condition, nor had even the smell of smoke clung to them.

Then Nebuchadnezzar said, "Blessed be the God of Shadrach, Meshach, and Abednego, Who has sent His angel and delivered His servants who believed in, trusted in, *and* relied on Him! And they set aside the king's command and yielded their bodies rather than serve or worship any god except their own God. Therefore I make a decree that any people, nation, and language that speaks anything amiss against the God of Shadrach, Meshach, and Abednego shall be cut in pieces and their houses be made a dunghill, for there is no other God who can deliver in this way!" (Daniel 3:24-30)

. . .

Then the king promoted Shadrach, Meshach, and Abednego in the province of Babylon. You see, sometimes things might happen to us that are not good, and it makes us want to ask, "What is going on here?" But the trial we're walking through might not even be about us —God could be trying to work something in our life that will bring other people to Him.

In this case, God worked through His obedient servants. Nebuchadnezzar's influence was everywhere because his kingdom was big. God allowed a situation to go forward because He had already decided to intercede in a dramatic way. These three guys believed in God, loved Him, and trusted Him. They had already said that God could rescue them from the king, but even if God didn't, they would still not bow down.

God allowed an event that brought a massive revelation of His glory and might on the scene in the physical realm. From the mouth of the leader came praise to God. The whole land would hear about this miracle, and the whole kingdom would know about God.

When we go through our own "walls of water" moments, they are meant for us to see God in a deeper way. But for others, these experiences plant seeds of faith. As Christians, we have a promise. The Bible says in Romans 8:28,

"And we know that all things work together for good to those who love God, to those who are the called according to *His* purpose." (NKJV)

God can deliver us from the hand of our foe and from any difficult situation we find ourselves in. But even if He doesn't, we are not bowing to fear, compromising, or whatever else the enemy would try to get us to do.

After this deliverance, Shadrach, Meshach, and Abednego would never be the same. The testimony these men no doubt shared might have encouraged countless people to keep going no matter the cost—even if it meant death. God was worth it.

When that bullet hit the ground in front of me, I did not see it floating mid-air like a scene from *The Matrix*. Instead, it whizzed toward me, made a thud sound like it had hit something, and bounced on the ground. To my amazement, when I looked down, there was a bare spot on the ground, and on that bare spot was the bent bullet. Because the bullet hit the ground so hard, it made what I can only describe as a concussion sound, and the ground seemed to bounce a little.

It was almost like the scene in *Jurassic Park*, when the T-Rex's approaching footsteps made the cup of water on the dashboard of the Jeep ripple. It moved because of the heaviness of the dinosaur walking, as he stepped down heavy and hard. The bullet hit the ground in a similar fashion-it stopped, fell to the ground and bounced once, landing on the ground again. This was a moment of divine intervention in my life.

Why did the Lord stop this tragedy from happening? There are plenty of other incidents in our lives where we had to get stitches, get a cast, etc. So why this one?

I might never know. There are going to be a lot of things that happen that will require us to have faith. God doesn't always reveal the reason why He does the things He does—we just have to believe that He works out all things for our good (Romans 8:28).

There were eyewitnesses that day to this miracle. Would you believe that it's a story I have not shared very often until now? I had to pull it from deep within my memory. Perhaps the Lord had me keep this story tucked away so I wouldn't get prideful and careless with my life. Maybe all of this is coming out right now for you, the reader, as well as for myself, to open up a whole new understanding of God's protection in our lives.

Maybe you have a similar story where God physically manifested His power in your life that you haven't shared. Perhaps God will pull it out later in your life as a testimony of Him walking with you so that you can use it to encourage others.

I know that one of God's angels was assigned to me that day, and

I'm grateful to be alive today. I am grateful that I'm not having to deal with any sort of cognitive issue because of a bullet that hit my head when I was fifteen.

The Lord indeed created a wall of water for me to walk through, right through the middle of the sea to the other side. I sit here on the couch writing, with my wife sitting close by and enjoying some relaxation as she works on her phone, and I recognize that miracle was for her too. We might not even be together nor have the wonderful family that we have if the Lord had not stepped in at that time.

**Practical Tips for Staying Focused on God in Hard Times**

When we find ourselves facing difficult circumstances, like Shadrach, Meshach, and Abednego, it can be tempting to give up or worry if God will come through. Here are some ways we can stay focused on God in hard times:

1. **Recall Past Interventions**
2. It helps to keep a journal of times when God clearly rescued or provided for you. Reflecting on these moments rekindles hope and reminds you He is still at work.
3. **Immerse Yourself in Scripture**
4. In moments of trial, reading or listening to the Word of God anchors your heart and mind in truth. Focus on promises like Romans 8:28 that testify to God's overarching goodness.
5. **Cultivate Worship and Thanksgiving**
6. Worship breaks the grip of anxiety and despair. Even a simple prayer of thanks, such as "God, You are faithful," can shift your perspective and invite His presence into your challenging situation.
7. **Seek Encouragement from Others**
8. Don't isolate yourself. Talk to trusted friends or mentors

who can pray with you. Hearing their testimonies and experiences can strengthen your faith in God's faithfulness.

9. **Surrender Outcomes to God**

10. Like Shadrach, Meshach, and Abednego, declare: "God can deliver me, but even if he doesn't, I will not bow." Trusting Him fully, even when you don't see immediate results, keeps you centered on His sovereignty and love.

## Prayer

Dear Heavenly Father, thank You for Your constant protection and provision in our lives. Help us to trust in Your plans and purposes, even when we cannot see the way forward. Strengthen our faith and guide us through life's challenges as we take comfort in the fact that You are always with us. In Jesus' name, amen.

# CHAPTER 5
# JOURNEY

---

WHAT MAN IS he who desires life *and* longs for many days, that he may see good?

Keep your tongue from evil and your lips from speaking deceit.

Depart from evil and do good; seek, inquire for, *and* crave peace and pursue (go after) it! (Psalm 34:12-14)

I grew up in a church environment. As a child, I would play "church," lining up my stuffed animals and preaching to them. From a young age, God had called me to ministry. I accepted Jesus as a child and rededicated my life as a teenager. While I never despised God, I walked through a time when I wasn't fully devoted to Him.

For years before I ever truly yielded everything to Jesus, I struggled in a cycle of sin, guilt, and repentance, only to fall back into temptation again. Around and around the crazy cycle would go. Despite my desire to live for God, I lacked the power to resist the pull of my flesh.

It wasn't until I found myself in deep trouble, desperately in need of rescue, that I realized I needed a radical change. God does allow trouble and uses it to help us look to Him for help—real help— before it's too late.

God had intervened in my life before, but this time, He required a transformation in me. He used my troubles as a wake-up call, nudging me back into a relationship with Him and His church–which I was not attending for years at that time. I began attending a Bible-centered church where I encountered fresh teachings on grace. During this period, I genuinely desired to renew my commitment to serving God. I wanted to break free from the grip of sin and the cycles I continuously found myself in. So, in my late twenties, I finally returned to God.

I believe human responses to God fall in the following categories: there are those who outright reject Him; those who love Him, but want to hang on to their sin; and those who truly love Him and detest sin but struggle to overcome it.

Unfortunately, many churches fail to teach believers about the power of the Holy Spirit, who empowers us to resist temptation. This is why the church in general needs to preach and teach the whole counsel of God as it relates to the work of the Holy Spirit. I was not taught previously about the power to live out the Christian walk that comes from this relationship with the Holy Spirit, and because of this lack of spiritual power, all I had was my self-will and personal strength to stand my ground.

Now, years later, I am convinced of the Holy Spirit's active role in our lives and teach others how to partner with Him to overcome sin.

•  •  •

**Surrendering to God's Will Brings Clarity and Purpose**

It is in surrender that we truly begin to see who God is and who we are called to be. When we let go of our own agendas, worries, and self-efforts, we create space for God to direct us.

This opens our eyes to a clarity we could never achieve on our own. Instead of being pulled in every direction by sin, guilt, or our own desires, we find purpose in God's plan. Surrendering to Him leads to real freedom, because God's will is not meant to imprison us. It's meant to release us into the fullest life possible—one that's marked by His grace and guidance.

In essence, when we align ourselves with His plan, uncertainty lifts off of us and we have more clarity. We are able to step forward with confidence, knowing we are walking on the path He designed just for us.

In those early days after I returned and started attending church, I found myself at a crossroads. If God didn't intervene, my life would have taken a disastrous turn. During a church service, as I stood in worship with tears streaming down my face, I heard Jesus urging me to surrender fully. "If you yield to Me, raise your hands," He said.

Though I came from a background where raising hands in worship wasn't customary, I obeyed. As I lifted my hands, I felt a powerful heat course through my body. It was an encounter with the Lord unlike I'd ever had before.

That moment marked a turning point in my life. There was no going back; I was committed to following God's path, no matter the cost.

A few weeks later, God gave me what I had never received before. I experienced the infilling of the Holy Spirit, which is a baptism of power that equipped me to live out the Christian life victoriously. There is a moment of salvation where the Holy Spirit seals us (for example, we take a drink from a cup). Then, there is asking for more. This asking the Lord to fill us with the Holy Spirit and receiving it is like being thrown in the ocean.

This baptism provides not only empowerment for service, but also a heightened awareness of God's presence, greater boldness in witnessing, and a deeper sensitivity to the Spirit's leading. It's not about achieving a spiritual status; it's about surrendering to God's transformative work and allowing His power to flow through us.

## A Journey of Transformation

Getting filled with the Holy Spirit marked the beginning of a transformative journey. God lifted me out of my trials and troubles. He created a "walls of water" environment for me to see Him and His mercy more clearly. God began to refine me, molding me into His Son's image. I grew immensely at a great Bible-believing church, and God used the preaching, teaching and leadership of a great pastor to continue to shape me.

God desires the best for our lives, but He also requires our obedience. We must align ourselves with His will and follow Him wholeheartedly.

From that moment on, God has continued to open doors and reveal His plans for my life. While the journey hasn't been without challenges, I've learned to trust in God's guidance and rely on His strength to see me through.

As I reflect on my journey, I'm reminded of the importance of seeking God's wisdom and following His lead. His Word provides the blueprint for a life of purpose and fulfillment—a path that leads to good days and abundant blessings.

As we seek to live according to God's Word, I pray that we would heed the wisdom of Psalm 34:12-14, striving for a life of righteousness and peace. I invite you to join me in a prayer of surrender, inviting Jesus to take the reins of your life and lead you on your own journey of faith.

## Prayer

Dear Heavenly Father, I desire to surrender to You. Please help me, Jesus. I want to love You and express my remorse for my sins and mistakes. I am turning away from my sins and repenting of them. I ask you to forgive me and cleanse me. Jesus, please come into my heart and my life and save me. I believe You are God's Son, who died on the cross for the sins of the world, including mine. I believe that God raised you to life again on the third day. Help me to live for You from this day forward, by the power of your Holy Spirit. Thank you, Jesus, for saving me. I love You. In Jesus' mighty name, amen.

If you prayed that prayer for the first time or prayed it as a rededication, please reach out to us! Even if you have to leave a message, one of our team members will call you back. You can reach our office at 254-655-2171.

Write to us PO Box 253 China Springs, Texas 76633.
You can also send an email to pastor@thechurchalive.com.

Don't delay—we want to help you on your journey with Jesus with some free materials. We also want to pray with you, and we would love to assist you in finding a life-giving, Bible-teaching church family near you.

# CHAPTER 6
# THE OTHER SIDE

---

Behold, I am doing a new thing! Now it springs forth; do you not perceive *and* know it *and* will you not give heed to it? I will even make a way in the wilderness and rivers in the desert. (Isaiah 43:19)

Part of my role as a pastor is to steadfastly maintain faith, consistently urging others (as well as myself) to "keep showing up" and to keep believing and trusting in God. While I'm aware that others have also encouraged us, the responsibility of carrying that mantle falls heavily on me as the leader. Undoubtedly, it's the Lord who ultimately strengthens us. He entrusts the leader with forging the trail.

One night, as our staff prepared for a night of worship, I found myself rather tired. I'm sure I'm not the only one who has felt overly tired before a church function. For some reason, this night I was particularly exhausted.

We were already aware that some folks wouldn't be attending, which didn't help morale. My lovely bride was assisting my mom with some medical appointments, which ran longer than expected and caused her to be behind schedule. Because of these things, I was seriously contemplating postponing the event to the following month.

Unless there's a compelling reason to do so, it's not characteristic of me to change an event once it's set, especially on such short notice. My associate pastor and his family arrived to set up the music, preparing to sing live. I confided in him about my struggle to muster the energy for the evening.

He responded, "We give the sacrifice of praise."

*Ugh.* I didn't need him to be Mr. Saint-not now. "Oh yes, of course," I replied. "Let's do this."

Despite my initial reluctance, we pressed on. As I entered the other room, I sensed that this night was significant for us. It's easy to forget, when you're a ministry leader, that the service and components of worship are also for you. We're producing for others, yet we ourselves need times of refreshing.

I felt remorse for the fact that I'd almost canceled. We began the service, and during it, I apologized to the Lord and asked for forgiveness for even considering canceling. I lifted my staff and declared the Word of the Lord anew, reiterating His promises for us.

I sought forgiveness from God for my exhaustion. His response was comforting: "You do not have to apologize for being tired." He knows and sees.

"Thank you, Lord, for your mercy." I responded.

. . .

**A Fresh Word**

Serving in the office of the prophet means the Lord will often use me to declare His Word. The Spirit prompted me to declare Deuteronomy 8, starting at verse 16 to the end of the chapter. These verses had been delivered to me a few years prior by another man of God, Rev. John Howarton. His fatherly words and encouragement have been timely and impactful throughout the years, especially during challenging times.

The Word, freshly issued for my family and for our church family, resonated deeply for me that night.

So you shall keep the commandments of the Lord your God, to walk in His ways and [reverently] fear Him.

For the Lord your God is bringing you into a good land, a land of brooks of water, of fountains and springs, flowing forth in valleys and hills; A land of wheat and barley, and vines and fig trees and pome-granates, a land of olive trees and honey; A land in which you shall eat food without shortage and lack nothing in it; a land whose stones are iron and out of whose hills you can dig copper.

When you have eaten and are full, then you shall bless the Lord your God for all the good land which He has given you.

Beware that you do not forget the Lord your God by not keeping His commandments, His precepts, and His statutes which I command you today, Lest when you have eaten and are full, and have built goodly houses and live in them, and when your herds and flocks multiply and your silver and gold is multiplied and all you have is multiplied, then your [minds and] hearts be lifted up and you forget the Lord your God, Who brought you out of the land of Egypt, out of the house of bondage,

Who led you through the great and terrible wilderness, with its fiery serpents and scorpions and thirsty ground where there was no water, but Who brought you forth water out of the flinty rock,  Who fed you in the wilderness with manna, which your fathers did not know, that He might humble you and test you, to do you good in the end.

And beware lest you say in your [mind and] heart, My power and the might of my hand have gotten me this wealth.

But you shall [earnestly] remember the Lord your God, for it is He Who gives you power to get wealth, that He may establish His covenant which He swore to your fathers, as it is this day.

And if you forget the Lord your God and walk after other gods and serve them and worship them, I testify against you this day

that you shall surely perish.

Like the nations which the Lord makes to perish before you, so shall you perish, because you would not obey the voice of the Lord your God. (Deuteronomy 8:6-20)

This is God's will for us, and God was using me to declare it again. He wanted us to know it and experience it, both the blessings and the consequences of obedience or disobedience.

We make room for our team and the church to develop in their gifting and calling, providing guidance when necessary. The Lord used another young lady from our leadership team to share a vision of the Father's hands over our physical home with a rainbow encircling it.

God is the originator of the rainbow. Although some have attempted to hijack it and associate it with other things, it has always been associated with God's promises, beginning with the promise He made to Noah never to flood the earth again (Genesis 9:11). No matter how much people try, any attempt to redefine it reveals a lack of understanding and life in Christ.

This vision of the Father's hands over our house, with His rainbow as a sign of His covenant, signifies our blood covenant with God. This was secured through Jesus and His sacrifice on the cross.

So, this worship night, the one I contemplated canceling, turned out to be a huge blessing and propelled us to the next level.

The presence of the Lord showed up and refreshed us all. He spoke to me personally in the corporate setting and reassured the group that was there of His plan for us. He settled our hearts yet again, allowing us to return to our peace as we continued to pursue Him. The night I wanted to postpone happened to be the night God did a mighty work in all our hearts!

This reminds me of Galatians 6:9, which exhorts us to not "lose heart and grow weary and faint in acting nobly and doing right, for in due time and at the appointed season we shall reap, if we do not loosen and relax our courage and faint."

God is faithful to fulfill His promises, and He demonstrates His power and wisdom as we journey forward. We're leaving the bank on one side of the river, the side behind us, and stepping out onto the other side, into a new, fresh place. But as we traverse this path, we're taking the time to truly experience God's power, kindness, wisdom, mercy, and love.

We must press on. We mustn't give up. We mustn't return to Egypt, which represents our former lives. What awaits us there? Memories of sin, failure, and shame. We need to prepare ourselves to fight the good fight of faith and stay in a place of faith when we find ourselves in stagnation. We don't know what blessing awaits us on the other side!

## Tools for Spiritual Warfare and Maintaining Faith

1. **Identify the Source of Attacks**
2. Recognize when exhaustion, discouragement, or fear may actually be part of the enemy's scheme to halt God's work. Step back, pray, and ask God for discernment.
3. **Claim God's Promises (Deuteronomy 8, Galatians 6:9, etc.)**
4. Scripture is our strongest weapon. Revisit passages that remind you of God's covenant, faithfulness, and the outcome of faithful obedience.
5. **Offer the "Sacrifice of Praise"**
6. Worship isn't just for Sunday mornings. When you feel worn out, choose to praise God anyway. This confounds the

enemy and rekindles your spirit (see 2 Chronicles 20:21–22 as an example of victory in praise).

7. **Stay Connected to Fellow Believers**
8. When I opened up to my associate pastor, he spoke truth to me at a moment when I was weak. Share your struggles with trusted people who can intercede, encourage, speak truth into your life, and remind you to keep praising God.
9. **Guard Against Complacency**
10. Whether things are going well or poorly, the enemy seeks any opportunity to derail us. Stay vigilant, keep your memory fresh on what God has done for you, and daily rely on His Word.
11. **Persevere in Prayer**
12. Persistent, consistent prayer keeps the lines of communication with God open. Even short, heartfelt prayers such as "Lord, help me" can anchor you in His presence.

## Prayer

Thank You, God, for Your faithfulness. You are the One who lifts my head and establishes me in Your love. Your ways are always best. Help me to accept your guidance in every area of my life more and more. Bless You, my Father. I love You, Jesus. Please help me to continue forward, in Jesus' name!

# CHAPTER 7
# THE SPECIAL KIND

_____

INDEED ALL WHO delight in piety *and* are determined to live a devoted *and* godly life in Christ Jesus will meet with persecution [will be made to suffer because of their religious stand]. (2 Timothy 3:12)

"Not everyone gets to go through these kinds of things," the Lord said to me during a particular season of my life. I had already left the world, repented of my former ways, and was earnestly seeking Him. There was nothing left in my old life to go back to, nor did I ever want to go back. I had committed myself to following Him, living out the Christian walk genuinely. I wanted to be the "real deal."

Yet I was struggling. It felt like there was an all-out war that had been waged against me. There were hours, days, and nights where it seemed like the enemy was committed to relentlessly bothering me. In many areas, I was resisting temptation, yet I still found myself battling questions about faith and God. At times, I felt overwhelmed by the wrestle.

Why was I having to endure all of this? I would cry out to God, saying, "Lord, I am trying to serve you. I am trying to live for you." What was happening? You may recall what the Word says in 1 Peter 4:1-3:

So, since Christ suffered in the flesh *for us, for you,* arm yourselves with the same thought *and* purpose [patiently to suffer rather than fail to please God]. For whoever has suffered in the flesh [having the mind of Christ] is done with [intentional] sin [has stopped pleasing himself and the world, and pleases God], So that he can no longer spend the rest of his natural life living by [his] human appetites *and* desires, but [he lives] for what God wills. For the time that is past already suffices for doing what the Gentiles like to do—living [as you have done] in shameless, insolent wantonness, in lustful desires, drunkenness, reveling, drinking bouts *and* abominable, lawless idolatries.

**Understanding the Spiritual War Against Our Soul**

There's a lot going on in these few verses, which ties directly to our theme of overcoming the enemy's lies. What's the point? When you're serious about living for God for real—no games, no joking, no compromises—there will be resistance. Those of us who want this new life in Christ will meet with persecution, most of which happens in the spiritual realm against our soul.

You may have already learned, read, or been taught that the soul is made up of our mind, our will, and our emotions. This area is where much of the spiritual resistance and attacks occur; not all, but much. We do have two other parts to our tri-part being: our spirit, which is what actually gets "born again" at salvation, and our body. Sometimes, the devil attacks our bodies with sickness and diseases, as he did in the book of Job.

The Lord allowed Job to be tested, but the enemy was the one behind it. When we decide to yield to the Lord and submit ourselves to Him, we become a great threat to the devil and such a wonderful prize for him if we fall. We now have a bullseye on us; we are "illuminated" as targets. I believe the enemy can see who is saved because we have the light of the Lord in us. Likewise, he also knows who is on his side.

He is the enemy of our soul, and he attacks our soul by targeting our mind. The book *Battlefield of the Mind* by Joyce Meyer helped me to understand this reality more clearly. This book emphasizes how the mind is the primary battlefield the enemy fights us on, and how mastering our thought life is critical for winning spiritual battles. The enemy is skilled at launching attacks through making suggestions and planting thoughts to bring us down.

Joyce Meyer exhorts us to "think about what you're thinking about."[3] We should be especially vigilant at monitoring our thoughts. Mastering our thought life is absolutely critical to winning the battles that are waged against us.

Our emotions are another door the enemy uses to bring persecution against us. Have you ever had a great day and yet found yourself in a bad mood? Maybe your spouse or friend might even have asked you what was wrong, and you honestly don't remember what happened. A negative thought was most likely sown in your mind, and without realizing it, you started to allow your mind to meditate on that thought. Doing this invited your emotions to the party. Not wanting to be left out, they joined and left you all bent out of shape.

· · ·

## Suffering in the Flesh vs. Living in the Spirit

Looking back at 1 Peter 4:1, we learn that since Christ suffered in the body, we should arm ourselves with the same purpose. Living a godly life is not something that happens by chance—it happens by choice.

There are those who teach and believe we are predestined and chosen to be saved. Unfortunately, this view removes all accountability. They claim that we don't have to worry about sin or salvation. In other words, we can just live any old way we want, with no regard to consequences. Yet the whole Bible shows us that we have an active role in our salvation and sanctification and must cooperate with God to grow up in Christ.

If we are truly predestined, and our own choices mean nothing, then the two Scriptures that I used in this chapter have no meaning.

God expects us to cooperate with Him to change our lives. The majority of the New Testament is about how to conduct ourselves once we're saved! It's about growing up and maturing. Philippians 2:12 says,

Therefore, my beloved, as you have always obeyed, not as in my presence only, but now much more in my absence, work out your own salvation with fear and trembling. (NKJV)

I like the way the Classic Amplified Bible reads,

Therefore, my dear ones, as you have always obeyed [my suggestions], so now, not only [with the enthusiasm you would show] in my presence but much more because I am absent, work out (cultivate, carry out to the goal, and fully complete) your own salvation with reverence *and* awe and trembling (self-distrust, with serious caution, tenderness of conscience, watchfulness against temptation, timidly shrinking from whatever might offend God and discredit the name of Christ).

. . .

Our salvation is a free gift of God to us; living it out is our gift to Him. Yes, Scripture mentions that God has "predestined us to be conformed to the image of Christ." Yet we must still choose to cooperate with the Lord. We can absolutely refuse to cooperate with the Lord, and it won't happen. There is free will in this operation; we must accept God's offer.

**Suffering with Christ: Denying the Flesh**

Since there is a place of eternal separation for those who want to get their way, and we know God desires for us to be saved, there certainly must be a free will in operation to choose whether we want to accept God's offer of salvation or not.

For example, I might decide that I want to take my child to get McDonald's ice cream and go to the park to play tomorrow afternoon, so I share this intention with my family. You could say I "predestined" these plans to happen tomorrow. However, I attach some stipulations to the condition, which is that each person has to do their chores and schoolwork before we go.

However, the next day, everybody wakes up. We get moving, and I notice that the kids are back talking and being disobedient. They don't get their chores or schoolwork done on time and there's a lot of grumbling and complaining about having to complete these tasks.

Although I had previously made plans to get ice cream and go to the park, the choices they made prevented this from happening. I had set the stipulations at the beginning, and they knew what they were. Thus, the reward was forfeited. Was it because I wanted them to forfeit it? Or was it because of their choices?

If I were to correlate this situation with the predestination debate, it would be as if my family were to conclude that I didn't want them to get ice cream or go to the park instead of them missing out as a result of their choices.

Since we have to cooperate with the Lord to have the life God wants us to have, it's important to understand that we will have to work on it. First Peter shows us that sometimes we must suffer in the body so we don't fail to please God. This can mean denying our flesh, which is a form of suffering.

The Bible instructs us to put to death the evil that lurks within us and to pick up our cross daily and follow the Lord. When we do this, the enemy often bombards us with temptation. We all have things in our lives that serve as temptations to us because they are pleasing to our flesh. The enemy suggests we engage in these things. Our brand-new self does not want to, however, and this is what produces the inward struggle. This tug-of-war, depending on its intensity, causes suffering.

When we choose to turn our lives to God, the enemy tries to persecute us for our godly stance. He bombards us, left and right, with temptation and other things to try to get us to fail. When we choose to say no, to stand up and not yield to the suggestions he throws our way, then we've chosen to pick up our cross and follow after the Lord. First Peter 4:4 adds,

They are astonished *and* think it very queer that you do not now run hand in hand with them in the same excesses of dissipation, and they abuse [you].

This verse speaks of the reactions from friends and family who can't fathom why we no longer participate in their indulgences. They may reject us, causing a form of suffering and persecution as well. Often, this path leads to loneliness, as we can lose people in our lives when we prioritize living for the Lord.

When I returned to the Lord and rededicated my life to Him, I no longer desired the activities I once enjoyed with my friends. Gradually, I found myself alone with Him, deepening my relationship with Him through prayer, worship, fellowship with other believers, and the

Word. This period, before I got married, allowed me to intimately know Him and become rooted in Him.

When the Lord told me "not everyone gets to go through these kind of things," I realized it's because not everyone is willing to fully surrender to Him. Not everyone will wrestle to live a life that honors God.

## A Calling

As a pastor, the nature of my position requires walking away from entrenched demonic strongholds and even from relationships that are unhealthy. Yet at some point, we all must decide whether to keep toxic friends or fully surrender to the Lord and allow Him to replace them.

We will always have free will and choice, and when we see God's true nature—His love, compassion, and care—it compels us to live for Him, even in the face of hardship.

God wants you to understand that if you're serious about this new life, He will intervene when necessary to guide and mature you. When He displays His power and glory, you'll see Him in a new light and realize you're not alone. He sees, hears, and is aware of your situation. So whether we live or die, we win if we're in Christ.

## Prayer

Dear Father, I come before You. Your grace has been abundant in my life, rescuing me time and time again. I am profoundly grateful for Your continuous intervention. I owe You my everything. Most of all, thank You for delivering me from the kingdom of darkness and transferring me into the kingdom of Your Son.

Lord, I humbly ask for Your guidance to walk in Your ways and to turn completely away from any and all sin. I desire to cooperate fully with Your Holy Spirit, becoming everything You desire me to be. In Jesus' name, amen.

# CHAPTER 8
# BACK ON THE COUCH

---

ROLL your works upon the Lord [commit and trust them wholly to Him; He will cause your thoughts to become agreeable to His will, and so shall your plans be established *and* succeed. (Proverbs 16:3)

It's late at night, and I find myself back on the couch in the living room. The time reads 11:09 p.m. We have a full day ahead tomorrow, with an early morning alarm set for 6 a.m.

Our evening activities are already complete. We've watched a family wind-down show, each of us has read our own individual devotional books, and we've done our devotional together to cap off the day. We are ready for bed, until it hits me.

"Oh no!" I exclaim.

"You forgot your hour," Misty says. She knows me so well.

"Yes."

I somehow managed to forget the hour I was supposed to spend working on this book, which was a crucial commitment I had made to the Lord on the 42-day fast I was on. During this particular fast, which I was doing Tuesday through Friday, I had dedicated time to work on this project each day. I knew that if I didn't set aside a dedicated time to write, I wouldn't get around to it.

**Stolen**

Part of how the enemy steals from us is through a life that is overflowing with busyness. We can get so preoccupied with other things that we never pursue our passions. Just think of how many things God has for us to do that we never get around to because we run out of time?

During this fast, I'm intentionally ensuring that this manuscript gets completed. It's about the act of completion for me right now. To listen to and obey Him is important, and I want to make sure I honor Him by doing what He has asked me to do. While I hope you will find benefit in these pages and I'm glad you have purchased this book, my obedience to Him in writing is, for me, the most important part.

There are many things that the Lord does for us that we cannot do for ourselves. But there are many more things He wants us to do. For example, God does not wash our laundry or clean our car for us. He expects us to take care of these things, since we are stewards of them.

Similarly, while He is not the one writing this book, He can give me the energy, knowledge, and strength to get it done. I am doing my part, and I am leaving the results in His hands.

## Getting it Done

Now, I'm sitting with a glass of grape juice in hand and my iPad on my lap, working on this manuscript. I have an hour more of work after clocking out for the night.

This fast is the longest one I've embarked on. This devotion is meant to bear fruit and move us forward.

However, I'm tired and my eyes are heavy. I'm hoping the Lord will give me permission to finish these next few sentences and allow me to go to bed. But I haven't heard anything yet, so I'll keep typing, watching the clock that seems to slow down to a crawl as the hour ticks by.

A wall of water might not part for me tonight, whisking me away to restful slumber. But I know from past experiences that God is capable of doing that. However, He may not do so tonight, and I love Him anyway. Perhaps He needs me to taste victory through the path right in front of me that I have to walk through rather than having a quick fix. By allowing me to be trained for the future, He is, in fact, providing walls of water for my future.

Tonight, I've been battling tiredness and the "I don't want to do this" mindset. If I were to give in and call it quits for the evening, what excuse would it be easier for me to make next time? Depression? Worry? Conflict? Doubt? Busyness? I made a commitment to the Lord during this fast, and I have to push aside the thoughts and feelings that cause me to want to stop.

What about you? Will you simply refuse to give the enemy any more time by worrying, doubting, or compromising? There are many battles we engage in, some of which never get off the ground as we mature and grow in warfare. We don't even need to give the time of day to the spirits of worry, fear, or anger, understanding that there are spirits assigned to these particular areas to attack us in.

These spiritual forces bombard us with negative thoughts, which, if left unchecked, can produce negative emotions, driving many of our actions that could set us up for failure.

If I had chosen to go to bed instead of staying true to my commitment to God, I would have been bothered all night with condemnation and woken up feeling bad for not doing what I had promised. I knew that would happen, so I refused to listen to the enemy and shook off my tiredness. It feels great to fight through and win. I trusted in Him, allowed Him to strengthen me, and finished what I started.

Not every victory is a dramatic water-parting event, but every victory is an experience with God where we can learn something about Him, gain new insight, and build new spiritual muscles. God wants all of us to have personal experiences with Him. That is His desire. Would you like to? If so, just say, "God, I want to know You more. I want to have the reality of Your presence in my life, even today!"


**Messed Up**


During another challenging season of my life, the Lord spoke to me and said, "Other great men of the Bible have gone through some of the same things you're going through."

My first response was, "Wow... Other great men! Lord, are you saying...?"

"That these men have gone through some of the same things."

"Really?"

I did not see myself as a great man. And I also did not consider that anything that I was experiencing could have been something anyone else, especially a great man, would have wrestled with.

## Building

God allows many of the circumstances we go through to build our character. As a Christian, character-building places a significant focus on faith. Satan fights against our faith, primarily through lies, half-truths, and complete deception.

Consider this in the context of this book: troubles come into our lives, and the enemy says this or that will happen. He says things like, "You're not going to make it" or "God will not show up this time." And then, God rescues you. He delivers you. God might have even spoken to you beforehand that He was going to help you, but the lies, as they always do, still came around.

Who are we going to believe? Are we believing God and His Word, or are we believing the enemy's words? Who is telling the truth?

There are usually three different voices in our heads at any given time: God's voice, the devil's voice, and our own voice. Learning to discern who is speaking to us is part of our maturing process and it's something absolutely imperative that we do. This is one of the primary reasons why learning God's Word so that it fills our hearts and minds is essential.

God inspired other "great men" throughout history to write down His words and put it in book form. Let's take a quick journey and side-track here. We will come back to the rest of this chapter in a moment.

## Divine Partnerships

The Bible is made up of 66 books: 39 in the Old Testament and 27 in the New Testament. There are many authors of these books. Some authors wrote more than one book, like the Apostle Paul, who wrote a good portion of the New Testament in the form of letters to the churches and others during that time.

A relative of mine got bent out of shape with me when talking about the Bible, and the same question came up when I was explaining something from the Scriptures. His argument was that men wrote it, not God.

Now I'm not saying that this relative is or was saved or not saved, but his mind was spewing out fleshly questions and reasonings. People who are not born again think fleshly thoughts because they have a fleshly mind. Because they do things in the flesh, without God's voluntary involvement, the things they do are done out of their own will.

I'd also like to mention that it's not a matter of whether God is able to use a human to write His words or not. You may wonder if God will use you or not. It's a matter of which side you will be on when He does. God can even work through the wicked to fulfill His wishes and plans. Yes, you still have free will. You can freely choose salvation, which leads to life, or being lost which leads to death. Romans 12:1-2 says this:

I appeal to you therefore, brethren, *and* beg of you in view of [all] the mercies of God, to make a decisive dedication of your bodies [presenting all your members and faculties] as a living sacrifice, holy (devoted, consecrated) and well pleasing to God, which is your reasonable (rational, intelligent) service *and* spiritual worship.

Do not be conformed to this world (this age), [fashioned after and adapted to its external, superficial customs], but be transformed (changed) by the [entire] renewal of your mind [by its new ideals and its new attitude], so that you may prove [for yourselves] what is the good and acceptable and perfect will of God, *even* the thing which is good and acceptable and perfect [in His sight for you].

We must renew our minds. And how do we renew our minds? By studying and meditating on the Word of God and applying it in our lives.

**Practical Steps for Renewing the Mind**

1. Identify ungodly or negative thoughts. Ask the Holy Spirit to make you aware of patterns in your thinking that conflict with Scripture—worry, fear, condemnation, and so forth. Write them down so you can address them directly.
2. Replace these thoughts with truth. Search the Bible for verses that directly counter the negative thought. For example, if you struggle with anxiety, cling to Philippians 4:6–7 which tells us to be anxious for nothing but pray about everything.
3. Meditate on key Scriptures. Spend time daily pondering, repeating, or writing out Bible passages that speak to your situation. Let them sink deeply into your heart and mind.
4. Speak the Word out loud. Confess biblical truths over yourself, your family, and your circumstances. Hearing the Word helps solidify it in your heart.
5. Pray for the Holy Spirit's help. Ask the Spirit to illuminate any area of your thinking that needs renewal and to strengthen you in applying the Word in everyday life.
6. Persist through setbacks. Renewing your mind is an ongoing process. If old thought patterns resurface, turn again to God's Word and prayer. Over time, you'll see growth and greater victory.

I responded to my relative calmly, letting him know that the people God worked through to pen the words of God were people completely submitted to His will. They were not people who were intentionally compromising. Of course, they weren't free from every mistake, but they did not practice sin as a lifestyle. These people allowed God to train them. They believed God, and He worked through them, giving them divine inspiration, to write down what He said.

God could have written these words Himself, like He wrote the Ten

Commandments on the stone tablets. But He did not do it this way. He chose, over time, to allow people to partner with Him to hear His voice and be inspired to write His words. And since these words are active and alive, they are full of self-fulfilling power to accomplish what God sent them out to perform.

We can say that John wrote the book of John. We can also say that God wrote the book of John. John was the vessel that God worked through. He was, if you will, the "physical pen." But God was the mind and heart expressing Himself through the willing "pen." Likewise, we are the vessels today for God to work many things through.

## The Mind of Christ

Do you ever journal while you are praying and studying the Bible or during your conversations with the Lord? If you do, do you ever feel like God opens up your understanding? Do you ever feel like you have a knowing in your heart, or an answer to your situation or question? Do you ever feel like God spoke something to you personally for your life and maybe something for someone else's life? I believe that is a small taste of God bringing inspiration by His Spirit into our lives.

In 1 Corinthians 2:16 we read, "For who has known the mind of the Lord that he may instruct Him? But we have the mind of Christ."

The men God inspired to write the content of these books and letters were yielded to God. He did the speaking, and they did the dictation. God's voice never contradicts His own Word, and He will not ask us to violate it.

If we hear a voice inside our head that breaks our peace or asks us to do something that goes directly against the Bible, it's not God's voice. There are many people whose lives have become messed up by doing something they thought God told them to do, but it was either the enemy or their own self. We cannot assume every voice we hear is the Lord. The Lord does speak to us, but the enemy speaks to us as well. We speak to ourselves also and sometimes carry on long conversations with ourselves!

. . .

## His Sheep

When we are true sheep of God's pasture, He speaks to us. We must learn to discern what is His voice from what comes from ourselves or from the enemy. John 10:26-27 says,

But you do not believe *and* trust *and* rely on Me because you do not belong to My fold [you are no sheep of Mine]. The sheep that are My own hear *and* are listening to My voice; and I know them, and they follow Me.

What are you hearing? And more importantly, which voice are you listening to and following? You can know this by examining your way of living. Are you living in peace and joy? Do you feel as though you are walking in righteousness?

We can be financially successful as far as the world system is concerned and our lives can still be empty. We can be popular or even an influencer on social media and still be empty.

Are you able to discern what God is speaking to you? His voice has to be the loudest and most important in your life. If you could examine your life, how much of what you are doing right now could you say He has told you to do? Following the wrong counsel can lead us into an unfruitful and unfocused life.

If you find yourself in need of constant rescue because of decisions that you are making, maybe it's time to examine where you've been taking your orders from. And if God has been stepping in to deliver you, He's allowing you to see His faithfulness and mercy towards you.

Even so, God doesn't want us to remain in a place where we continuously need deliverance. Just as a loving parent would want their child to grow up, God likewise wants us to mature.

Maturity requires that we must ask ourselves who are we listening to and who is giving us advice. Who is the senior voice in our lives? Is our own voice calling all the shots? If we look at Psalm 1:1, we see that those who listen primarily to the Lord and do His will are happy and prosperous.

Blessed (happy, fortunate, prosperous, and enviable) is the man who walks *and* lives not in the counsel of the ungodly [following their advice, their plans and purposes], nor stands [submissive and inactive] in the path where sinners walk, nor sits down [to relax and rest] where the scornful

[and the mockers] gather.

As this verse notes, there is a reward in listening to God, following His plan, and shunning the counsel of the ungodly. This is why the people we used to hang around often have trouble understanding why we're not participating in their bad decisions and sinful living, and they even find it strange that we're following God. While they would love to get us to participate with them, we simply can't. Those who don't belong to God don't listen to His voice, but we are God's sheep, and He is our good Shepherd. It's His voice we must follow.

Remember that God sees every choice to listen to Him and follow Him, however small. Just because you're not seeing a dramatic, miraculous event every single day doesn't mean the Lord isn't working behind the scenes or that you're not doing the right thing. Keep pressing forward in faith, trusting that He is orchestrating things in ways you cannot see.

In moments when obedience seems tough or sacrifice feels too heavy, hold onto God's promises. We walk by faith, not by sight (2 Corinthians 5:7), knowing that He is always with us and never leaves us alone in our journey. As you align your thoughts and actions with God's Word, He will transform each step of obedience you take into a divine appointment, shaping your future and your character for his glory.

**Prayer**

Jesus, all glory and honor truly belong to You. Without You and what You've done for me, I'd be in real trouble. Thank You for Your mercy and grace. Thank You for helping me continue to fight the good fight of faith. Please continue to guide me and give me strength to keep going. In Jesus' name, amen.

# CHAPTER 9
# BUT GOD!

---

FOR WE DO NOT WANT you to be uninformed, brethren, about the affliction *and* oppressing distress which befell us in [the province of] Asia, how we were so utterly and unbearably weighed down *and* crushed that we despaired even of life [itself].

Indeed, we felt within ourselves that we had received the [very] sentence of death, but that was to keep us from trusting in *and* depending on ourselves instead of on God Who raises the dead.

[For it is He] Who rescued *and* saved us from such a perilous death, and He will still rescue *and* save us; in *and* on Him we have set our hope (our joyful and confident expectation) that He will again deliver us [from danger and destruction and draw us to Himself]…

(2 Corinthians 1:8-10)

*But God.*

These two small words may seem insignificant, but they hold tremendous hope and promise for us. We may have found ourselves in bad situations: "But God." He stepped in and brought deliverance to us.

As we think about what the enemy has tried to do to bring us to an utter end emotionally, mentally, spiritually and even physically, how many times has God stepped in so that he would not succeed?

Do you have your own "but God" story? Maybe you've experienced a time when the enemy whispered in your ear, "This time you won't make it," "This time the finances won't be there," "This time the medical report will show bad news," or "This time there will not be enough." Yet, you prayed. You held out hope. You believed that God could, and you were able to say back to all the lies of the enemy, "*But God* can do the impossible."

God always makes a way for His people. He has done so before, and He will continue doing so. You may be tempted to question, "God helped me before. God delivered me before. But will He really do it again?"

He will!

If you have children, think about how many times you've stepped in to help them. How many times have they become stuck in situations? Or how many times have they ended up in a circumstance because of their ignorance, youth, or lack of understanding?

As a parent, you desire to lift them up, not withholding mercy, even when they've made mistakes. Likewise, there are times when the enemy orchestrated circumstances to harm them even when they weren't seeking trouble. In these moments, do we intervene and help them? Of course we do. Does God also intervene? Of course He does!

In 2 Corinthians 8:10, Paul was expecting the Lord to rescue them in their current situation and believed the Lord would do it again in the future. There might have been a time in your life when the enemy sought to bring about your utter destruction. Perhaps you made mistakes that led to that point, or maybe you were unfairly accused. Regardless, you found yourself in a situation where prayer was your only option.

Shadrach, Meshach, and Abednego had a "but God" moment. The enemy threatened to burn them to death, but God intervened. The enemy doesn't have the final say; Jehovah has the final say. These men refused to abandon their faith, believing in God's goodness. They knew that even if deliverance didn't come in this world, they'd be rescued in the next.

There are times when we don't see God come through like we expect Him to. Can you believe and cling to Him if He doesn't deliver you in your situation as you expect Him to? I firmly believe that in any circumstance we find ourselves in, we can declare to the enemy, "But God has the final say!"

God intervenes in miraculous ways. He can cause your bills to be paid, cure sicknesses, restore hopeless relationships, and protect from accidents. His power is profound.

I encourage you to reflect on moments in your life, "walls of water" moments, when God did the impossible. Share these stories of deliverance with others, because they refresh and strengthen our faith. I will say it again—share, share, share these testimonies!

Often, these "but God" or "walls of water" moments aren't just about being delivered from the immediate crisis we find ourselves in. These moments are also key in our sanctification, as God uses them to refine us to look more like Christ. When we face the impossible and God steps in, we learn firsthand about His faithfulness, His compassion, and His power.

Each miraculous rescue builds in us a stronger foundation of faith. As we remember past deliverances, our confidence in God's ability to save us grows and makes us less susceptible to the enemy's lies. Just as the some of Israelites were shaped by their Red Sea experience, our own "walls of water" moments teach us obedience, gratitude, and humility. Trials reveal areas of weakness, and God uses them to form Christlike character in us.

The more we see God intervene, the more we realize we don't have to give in to worry and fear. Sanctification involves surrendering our plans and fears, trusting that if God can part a sea once, He can, and will, do it again. Experiencing God's deliverance firsthand equips us to comfort and encourage those going through similar struggles. We become conduits of His grace, telling others, "God did this for me, and He can do it for you, too."

When we're able to see the sanctifying effects of our "walls of water" moments, we see that every trial God brings us through has a greater purpose than we initially realize.

## Prayer

Dear Lord, thank You for doing what no one else can do. You perform the impossible for us, showing Your love and mercy. Help us deepen our commitment to You, trusting in Your goodness even when circumstances seem dire. In Jesus' name, amen.

# CHAPTER 10
# ONSET

---

WITHSTAND HIM; be firm in faith [against his onset—rooted, established, strong, immovable, and determined], knowing that the same (identical) sufferings are appointed to your brotherhood (the whole body of Christians) throughout the world. (1 Peter 5:9)

This opening Scripture refers to our enemy, who is the mutual foe of the entire body of Christ and the world. It also shows that no one is immune to his harassment. Each of us will experience his work in some way.

What is "his work?" What is his mission, so to speak? The Bible tells us in John 10:10 that "the thief comes only in order to steal and kill and destroy…".

The enemy is known as the father of lies because he is a deceiver. He lies to us, bringing deception into our minds to derail us from God's will for our lives. He aims to kill our dreams, physically harm us, and destroy our lives and futures.

For instance, he might deceive us into taking harmful substances, attempting to convince us that they'll make us feel better. Or he might coax us into excessive drinking, having convinced us that we somehow "deserve" it or that it's harmless. He could manipulate us emotionally to the point where we harm ourselves impulsively. Some of his tactics may not yield immediate consequences, but they gradually damage our bodies.

The bottom line is that we all have the same enemy who seeks to destroy our lives and futures. What does God instruct us to do concerning him? First Peter 5:9 tells us to "Withstand him; be firm in the faith [against his onset]."

God does not want us to tolerate the works or wiles of the devil in our lives. We are called to learn and mature to a place where we are actively resisting him at the onset, not allowing him to gain a foothold in our lives, no matter what situation we find ourselves in.

### Submission and Resistance

James 4:7 says that we are to "be subject to God. Resist the devil [stand firm against him], and he will flee from [us]." We must submit to God's way of doing things!

During the writing of this chapter, our church's Sunday morning stream was having technical issues. For a ministry that's heavily reliant on reaching people through the "airwaves," such a problem is significant.

We weren't sure which component was malfunctioning. If you think about all the moving parts in a broadcast, it's a wonder any of it functions at all! You have wi-fi, which alone is an engineering marvel. Then you must ensure smooth communication between computer hardware and software, along with ensuring your camera and audio systems cooperate. All these codes and signals converge on your main computer for processing, then get sent to a streaming company for distribution. A successful broadcast is determined by all of these things working together, so when something fails, it's a big problem.

We tried replacing software, purchasing a new camera, resetting the main computer, reinstalling systems.

"Great, the computer booted correctly. The camera seems to be detected, excellent!" "Our software update is functioning, and we're connected, fantastic!" It seemed like we were back in business...until Saturday late afternoon, during a system test—almost a week after the problem began.

Suddenly, sirens blared—"Error Alert, Error Alert! Failure, Failure!" Nothing worked!

God, why? You called us to "take the airwaves." You wanted us to broadcast, and Sunday mornings are crucial. Had He changed his mind without telling us?

All these questions and frustrations surfaced. Just a few days before on a Wednesday evening. The same Wednesday we talked about in a previous chapter. The Lord had reaffirmed His covenant with us and this ministry. He reiterated His will for us to establish a media ministry and take the airwaves. When He said this, I had felt in my heart that our equipment was going to need an upgrade. Up to this point, we were using hand-me-down items, some of which were barely functioning.

**Embracing Change and Facing the Enemy's Distractions**

I was the one resisting change, holding onto outdated equipment and trying to make do with patchwork solutions. Being thrifty is commendable, but sometimes, pieced-together solutions simply won't suffice. Perhaps, at times, the Lord desires for us to have something better rather than what we're using to just get by.

No matter what I did—trying to fix our equipment, change the software, or "make it work," it wasn't working. It seemed as if the Lord wasn't going to allow it. Could it be that He was allowing this situation to happen so He could bring a breakthrough?

God leads us in ways we may not understand. If we're slow to grasp His intentions or resist change, He may allow situations to cease functioning for no apparent reason other than to get our attention.

While the enemy attacks us through delays, hindrances, distractions, stealing, killing, and destroying, we are not to allow him to prevail. While he may cause problems and hinder our progress, God can actually turn these situations around for our good. He uses these situations to mature us.

God worked all things out for our good, and we still obtained top-notch, upgraded streaming equipment, even if it was the enemy's attempt to derail our ministry. In the end, God made us better off than we would have been if the enemy had just left us alone.

The "walls of water" deliverance, in this situation, wasn't in obtaining the new equipment. Instead, the parting of the water and the deliverance occurred within my understanding that God wanted to change things for us. It was in understanding that God was doing something for us that we needed for our ministry to reach the next level.

When you experience these moments in your life, where you witness God's loving, gracious hands and His personal involvement, it deepens your love and commitment to Him.

## Reality of the Enemy

The enemy does indeed attack and cause problems in our lives. He's a being who is the personification of evil. He has a mind and will as well as numerous allies, who joined him in a great rebellion against God.

God created a place separate from Himself, His kingdom, the holy angels, and the redeemed of the Lord, for these creatures. Their final destination is an awful, horrendous, almost unimaginable place.

There are times when we're so deceived and overwhelmed that we need God to miraculously rescue us. We need the sea to part so we can survive.

But as we develop and learn, God wants us to grow to a point where He doesn't need to reach down and save us as often as He did before. Just as a parent doesn't need to rescue their ten-year-old as frequently as their two-year-old, we need to grow and learn to walk in our God-given authority in the Spirit, resisting the enemy and his lies before a full-blown crisis hits.

Temptation from the devil, as the Lord once explained to me, is just "a suggestion." That was a ground-breaking insight for me! Temptations are just suggestions. It made more sense! We have an enemy who goes around making suggestions about what we should or shouldn't do, leading us into deception. But as James 4:7 exhorts us, we are to "resist him" (the devil) and we are promised that he will "flee from us."

## Why We Stay on Guard

Can you imagine heaven without the devil? There wouldn't be temptations or accusations. How many things would we not need a water-parting moment for if evil wasn't present? But while evil is still here, God is training us and growing us to understand that with Him, we can stop things before we get to the point of needing a rescue.

Having a "walls of water" moment is about God delivering us in the midst of a difficult situation and opening our eyes to Him in a new way, learning to be confident in Him and His power. Yet there's another layer: how we develop before the conflict spirals out of control. First Peter 5:8 says,

Be well balanced (temperate, sober of mind), be vigilant *and* cautious at all times; for that enemy of yours, the devil, roams around like a lion roaring [in fierce hunger], seeking someone to seize upon *and* devour.

The devil looks for a moment of weakness in you—a time when you let down your shield and aren't paying attention to the side attack. Sometimes it's after a victory, when we let our guard down and get blindsided. This is why the Bible exhorts us to be on guard (1 Peter 5:9).

I have actually experienced failure right after a victory several times.

It's like—YES! I won that battle. It was long, rough, and felt like it was going to last forever. If you've ever experienced a battle that felt like it had no end in sight, you know what I'm talking about.

Maybe at some particular moment, the Lord said something to you that gave you strength. Or perhaps there was a moment when holy anger rose up in you, and with his help (again), you were able to break through to victory…only to find yourself in a place of failure.

These moments are frustrating and can make us want to give up. But remember that it's only a permanent failure if you quit!

We must stay on guard, especially right after a breakthrough. We are more vulnerable in these moments, as our attention is usually elsewhere. We're not looking for an attack—after all, we just won! But the Bible does say to be on guard. We must keep an eye out, even when we get a win, so that you can continue to enjoy the victory!

Let's continue:

Withstand him; be firm in faith [against his onset—rooted, established, strong, immovable, and determined], knowing that the same (identical) sufferings are appointed to your brotherhood (the whole body of Christians) throughout the world."

And after you have suffered a little while, the God of all grace [Who imparts all blessing and favor], Who has called you to His [own] eternal glory in Christ *Jesus*, will Himself complete *and* make you what you ought to be, establish *and* ground you securely, and strengthen, and settle you. (1 Peter 5:9-10)

Resisting the devil at his onset is crucial. The main weapon he uses against us is deception, and he tries to steal from us, kill us, and destroy us with lies. Yet 2 Corinthians 10:4-6 reminds us that the weapons of our warfare are mighty in God for demolishing strongholds. We are to refute every thought, argument, or reasoning that comes to our minds and stands in contrast to the truth of God's Word.

Let us reread that passage:

For the weapons of our warfare are not physical [weapons of flesh and blood], but they are mighty before God for the overthrow *and* destruction of strongholds, [Inasmuch as we] refute arguments *and* theories *and* reasonings and every proud *and* lofty thing that sets itself up against the [true] knowledge of God; and we lead every thought *and* purpose away captive into the obedience of Christ (the Messiah, the Anointed One), Being in readiness to punish every [insubordinate for his] disobedience, when your own submission *and* obedience [as a church] are fully secured *and* complete.

So on one hand, God wants to show us, through deliverance, that He is there with us. He sees us, knows what's going on, and will step in and help us so we can know Him better. On the other hand, He wants us to be able to grow to a place where, with His help, we can avoid an all-out conflict in our soul by resisting the enemy's lies at the onset!

And finally, Ephesians 6:10-21 exhorts us to put on the whole armor of God so that we can be successful against the devil's strategies and deceptions. The truth is, we are wrestling against an enemy we cannot see, and we need the wisdom of God to be able to win this type of warfare.

For we are not wrestling with flesh and blood [contending only with physical opponents], but against the despotisms, against the powers, against [the master spirits who are] the world rulers of this present darkness, against the spirit forces of wickedness in the heavenly (supernatural) sphere. Therefore put on God's complete armor, that you may be able to resist *and* stand your ground on the evil day [of danger], and, having done all [the crisis demands], to stand [firmly in your place].Stand therefore [hold your ground], having tightened the belt of truth around your loins and having put on the breastplate of integrity *and* of moral rectitude *and* right standing with God, And having shod your feet in preparation [to face the enemy with the firm-footed stability, the promptness, and the readiness produced by the good news]of the Gospel of peace. Lift up over all the [covering] shield of saving faith, upon which you can quench all the flaming missiles of the wicked [one]. And take the helmet of salvation and the sword that the Spirit wields, which is the Word of God. (Ephesians 6:10-21)

It takes time to unbind someone who's been in bondage, just as God needed to show the Hebrews His power because they had been enslaved for 400 years. Sometimes it takes time; be patient with God and yourself as He develops you.

**Maturing in Our Walk**

Our hope is that God will help us grow up so we won't always need Him to part the seas as He once did. We want to grow in the Lord and develop knowledge, understanding, wisdom, and good stewardship so that our lives aren't marked by a constant need for deliverance. In this place, we experience much more peace, even as we hold on to the valuable lessons and the knowledge we gained from our "walls of water" experiences. To walk in the authority God has given us, allowing Him to teach us to stand firm and snuff out the enemy's threats at the onset, is a much more peaceful way to live.

**Strategies for Resisting Temptation at the Onset**

1. **Recognize the trigger.** When you sense yourself getting emotional about something or you find yourself in a mental battle, ask the Holy Spirit to help you identify the moment your mind first drifted toward sin or despair. Awareness is the first defense and knowing the open door the enemy came through helps you to be able to shut it.
2. **Confront the lie with Scripture.** Just as Jesus did (Matthew 4), quote God's Word to counter the enemy's suggestion. Be willing to let go of any lie you chose to believe and, with the help of the Holy Spirit, embrace God's truth.
3. **Use your spiritual weapons.** Pray immediately, focus on God's Word, and if possible, reach out to a trusted believer for support. Also, it's important to recognize that the sooner you let go of the lie or deal with the open door, the better.
4. **Shift your focus.** Temptation thrives when we dwell on it, so focus your mind on the truth and on other positive things. Lies start to lose their power when they are not being focused on.

5. **Stand firm and don't quit!** Even if you slip, get back up. If you find yourself focusing on the temptation, follow the above steps again. Lean on the help of the Holy Spirit and don't give in to the enemy's condemnation.

## Prayer

Father, thank You for preserving me this far in Jesus by Your Holy Spirit. Thank You that You did not let the battles go beyond what I could bear. Lord, I ask that You continue to help me grow up in my salvation. Please help me to also help others along the way. I pray that Your hand of protection would cover me and my loved ones. Please help those who do not know you to come into a place where they are willing to listen and hear. I love You and need You. In Jesus' name, amen.

# CHAPTER 11
# GOD'S FAITHFULNESS IN EVERY SEASON

---

And we know that all things work together for good to those who love God, to those who are the called according to *His* purpose. (Romans 8:28 NKJV)

Throughout this book, you have witnessed God's unwavering faithfulness as seen in Job's story, the deliverance of Shadrach, Meshach, and Abednego, the personal testimonies of miraculous intervention, and the ongoing guidance of the Holy Spirit. Each season of trial and triumph has revealed God's steadfast love and presence.

Think back to the "walls of water" moments you've explored.

- How God met you in the middle of an impossible situation, as He did with the Israelites at the Red Sea or Joshua's generation crossing the Jordan.
- How personal miracles, like surviving what could have been a tragedy, have highlighted the Lord's protective hand in your life and proved that you are never alone.
- How God allowed trials, as He did in Job's life, but even so, no scheme of the enemy could outdo His redemptive and restorative power.
- How my personal story of the bullet miracle demonstrated God's intervention, stopping what could have been and early death in its tracks and reminding us that His care extends even into "sudden danger" situations.
- How simple "but God" moments demonstrate that even when the enemy says you won't make it, the Lord steps in to deliver.
- How fervent prayer, commitment, renewing your mind in God's Word, and taking practical steps of wisdom can fend off the enemy's lies before they take root.

Every one of these episodes, from biblical heroes to modern-day testimonies, points to the same conclusion: *the same God who rescued people thousands of years ago is the same One who will bring you through trials in your personal life.* He will use every season of difficulty to refine your faith, build your character, and take your relationship with Him to another level.

When God said to me, "Other great men of the Bible have gone through some of the same things you're going through," I didn't understand that the trial I was facing was not unique. In essence, God allowed me to go through this as He was building me up, molding and shaping me into the image of His Son.

And yes, there were absolutely times I needed a "walls of water" deliverance from Him. He allowed me to have those times, too, to see Him in a much more intimate way.

He wants us to learn to trust Him, rely on Him, believe Him, and be careful who we are listening to. Even if your trial comes from the devil, God will still work out all things for good if you continue to walk by faith and cooperate with His Spirit.

And if our trial is of God's doing, then there is something He is allowing us to overcome. Who can stop Him? And why would we want to, if we know that He is good and works all things together for our good?

God is incredibly capable of delivering us, and not only delivering us, but also providing intimate knowledge of Himself during these times. In the act of the rescue, God's revelation of His goodness and gentleness is so perfect.

In every breakthrough and every victory we will ever have, God is at the end of it all, opening up away for us. And if He is, we owe Him our everything! In Romans 12:1-3, Paul declares:

I beseech you therefore, brethren, by the mercies of God, that you present your bodies a living sacrifice, holy, acceptable to God, *which is* your reasonable service. And do not be conformed to this world, but be transformed by the renewing of your mind, that you may prove what *is* that good and acceptable and perfect will of God.

Let us listen to Him and reap the benefit of doing so.

## Prayer

Father, thank You for helping me to hear Your voice above all others. Please help me to continue to learn Your ways, and to listen to, heed, love, and obey Your commands. Thank You for helping me overcome so many things in my life. I look forward to continuing my relationship with You now and into the eternities of eternities. In Jesus' name, amen.

# CHAPTER 12
# REMEMBER

---

AND YOU SHALL [EARNESTLY] REMEMBER ALL the way which the Lord your God led you these forty years in the wilderness, to humble you and to prove you, to know what was in your [mind and] heart, whether you would keep His commandments or not. (Deuteronomy 8:2)

We're at the end, but it's not the end. I imagine that God has already created "walls of water" moments for you, perhaps more than just once. If you've ever experienced times of uncertainty or despair, you're not alone. Just read the book of Psalms and see David's feelings and prayers; they are truly inspiring and encouraging.

We have an enemy who wants to blind us to God's incredible rescues and to ignore His involvement in our lives. He aims to undermine our confidence, and ultimately, our faith, trying to drown us in grief, distractions, and hopelessness.

But not you, and not anymore! Why? Because through the help of the Holy Spirit, you are going to remember the times when God rescued you, when He stepped in and interceded for you, when He created a "walls of water" moment.

## Remembering God's Faithfulness

You are also going to remember God's faithfulness, even when it seemed He was leading you through a trial instead of just rescuing you out of it immediately. Your testimony is, "God, thank You for Your help. Despite the enemy's attempts to take me out, by Your mercy and grace, I am still here!"

God is on your side, cheering you on to the finish line, encouraging you to stay the course with Him and finish the race set before you!

The word "remember" carries a lot of weight for your future success. If we recall His previous involvement in our lives, it will be easier to hold on for the Lord's help and not give up the next time hardship comes.

## The Sanctification Process

I had come back to the Lord and had been living for him for a good while, giving the Christian walk my best shot. Although certainly not perfect, I was on my way up and out of a lot of sinfulness. A pastor friend once said that when you come to the Lord and are saved or have rededicated your life to Him, you don't instantly become sinless, but you should "sin-less."

The Holy Spirit's job is to sanctify us, which is the process of sanctification. The Lord works in us as we cooperate with Him to change our lives, helping us to learn His ways and obey Him. We develop and mature as a Christians, just as two-year-olds grow and develop as their parents teach them. This is a representation of the sanctification process, which God must be allowed to do in us to help us grow.

## Redline: Intense Spiritual Warfare

As I was saying, when I came back to the Lord. It marked a "true" turning point; no half-hearted commitment, but a dedication to be all-in for God. During this time, I went through a very difficult season of spiritual warfare where I felt that the enemy was persistently bombarding my mind with lies that I couldn't quite seem to overcome.

During this season, when I would have visitors at my home, the enemy would harass my soul so intensely that I'd have to excuse myself to go to the bathroom. In the bathroom, I'd kneel before the Lord and seek the strength to stand back up. I would literally get on my knees on the bathroom floor and pray for clarity and calm. Unfortunately, this became a normal event. Once I felt spiritually strong enough again, I would rejoin my guests.

This was a severe season of spiritual warfare. The enemy would assail me with thoughts throughout the day and would even infiltrate my dreams.

I was so scared some nights that I did not want to sleep in my room. At that time, I was living alone. My faith was put to the test, as the war raged against me. Even though I had turned my life over to God, I was not immune from the enemy's attacks.

The Lord allowed these battles. He did not immediately end these attacks but walked with me through them. The physical, emotional, spiritual, and mental pressure, along with the fear, was so great that much of my chest hair turned white. It has remained mostly that way ever since. This period left a physical mark on my body as a reminder of what I had to endure.

Not everything is caused by sin, and we don't always experience the enemy's harassment because we opened a door to him. There are times when God orders it, which is what I experienced during that season. It was not failure or the result of or the consequences of sin I was dealing with. On the contrary, it's because my mind was set to obey. God can order times like these for our growth, and each person's experience is so different.

God allowed me to walk through this for His future glory. And here I still am, with my hand in God's. I love Him, and I am glad He led me through that period so that I could share this message with you!

## God-Directed Trials

Jacob was another person who was left with a physical mark after a trial. When he wrestled with the angel of the Lord, the angel touched the hollow of Jacob's thigh, and he had a limp for the rest of his life. He was allowed to have this as a mark of this event. Genesis 32:24-31 says,

And Jacob was left alone, and a Man wrestled with him until daybreak. And when [the Man] saw that He did not prevail against [Jacob], He touched the hollow of his thigh; and Jacob's thigh was put out of joint as he wrestled with Him.

Then He said, Let Me go, for day is breaking." But [Jacob] said, "I will not let You go unless You declare a blessing upon me."

[The Man] asked him, "What is your name?" And [in shock of realization, whispering] he said, "Jacob [supplanter, schemer, trickster, swindler]!"

And He said, Your name shall be called no more Jacob [supplanter], but Israel [contender with God]; for you have contended *and* have power with God and with men and have prevailed.

Then Jacob asked Him, Tell me, I pray You, what [in contrast] is Your name? But He said, Why is it that you ask My name? And [the Angel of God declared] a blessing on [Jacob] there.

And Jacob called the name of the place Peniel [the face of God], saying, For I have seen God face to face, and my life is spared *and* not snatched away. And as he passed Penuel [Peniel], the sun rose upon him, and he was limping because of his thigh.

You might be in the fight of your life, feeling like it will never end, just as I was. At the time, I felt as if I would never get to the end of the battle. I hoped, prayed, and begged the Lord to rescue me. Yet even though the battle continued, He did bring relief and He did strengthen me.

I couldn't see the bigger picture in those spiritual formative years, but He could. We can take the revelation we get from every "walls of water" moment with Him and encourage many others with them, helping them to also get the breakthrough they need.

I believe God allowed me to walk through that season of pressure, even though I'm not sure I'd want to do it again. He allowed a physical mark to be on my body as a reminder of what I had to walk through, to have a testimony of my experience with God's training.

The Lord never took His hand off me. If He had, I would not be here. We might think we can defeat the enemy in our own power—fat chance. It is God who gives us the strength to withstand him. As Luke 10:19 declares,

Behold! I have given you authority *and* power to trample upon serpents and scorpions, and [physical and mental strength and ability] over all the power that the enemy [possesses]; and nothing shall in any way harm you.

. . .

I would not trade the "walls of water" moments with God for anything. Looking back, I can also say in hindsight that I'm grateful for the times when the waters wouldn't part and I wasn't sure He would come through. It's these experiences that have shaped my faith.

## Stand Back Up

Sometimes you have to get quiet and kneel before the Lord to be able to stand back up. Have you ever experienced this? God wants to teach us to stand up to the enemy's lies, heal us, and help us to remain steadfast in Him. Without Him, we are simply no match for the enemy, who masquerades himself as an angel of light.

Our nature is no longer like the enemy's. Once we are born again, our nature in Christ changes. We want to do good and right. We don't really want to be bad or sin, even though sometimes we don't choose right. But God, in His mercy, sees all and knows all.

Whatever place you find yourself in, don't give up, don't lay down, and don't surrender to anyone but the Lord. God may be ready to send that "wall of water" moment for you that will change your life, and you will see the majesty of the Lord in His love and power.

Maybe He already has, and you feel as though you missed it. Maybe you did not remember the Lord as you should have. But if you desire to learn from this and want another chance, God will be more than gracious to redeem this opportunity.

Pray and ask God to forgive you. Be honest, be open, and don't hide your mistakes from Him. He knows anyway, but He needs you to acknowledge them. If you will, and allow Him to change your life, He will! Paul wrote in Philippians 3:13-14:

Brethren, I do not count myself to have apprehended; but one thing *I do,* forgetting those things which are behind and reaching forward to those things which are ahead,  I press toward the goal for the prize of the upward call of God in Christ Jesus.

. . .

Look at Jesus. Look at hope. Look at your destiny. And live!

## Prayer

Father in the name of our Savior Jesus Christ, thank you for every "wall of water" moment in our past. Thank you for parting the seas during trials and thank You that even in times that You didn't, You were teaching us to lean on You and trust You. We praise You for every rescue, every divine intervention, and every trial through which we've grown.

God, thank you for saving me. Thank You for raising me. Thank You for training me. Thank You for helping me. Lord, please help me to live for You, by the power of Your Holy Spirit, for the rest of my life. Please work through me to help others to win their fights and finish their races. God, if it was not for You, where would I be? Lord, help me to remember Your hand upon me and to walk in humble confidence before You for the rest of my life.

I thank You that I can look toward the future with hope. Whatever walls of water may appear, I trust that You will be with me in the midst of it, waiting to show me out and give me greater revelation of who You are. Prepare my heart to stand in faith, expecting Your deliverance. Thank You for walking with me, now and into eternity. In Jesus' name, amen.

# CHAPTER 13
# WRAP-UP

---

DEAR READER,

Thank you for investing your time in reading this book. Though we may never meet face-to-face, I hope that the words within these pages have been a source of blessing and encouragement to you. My prayer is that you've found something relatable and that the Lord has touched your heart in some way.

I want you to know that I love you, and more importantly, God loves you unfailingly. He has a divine plan and purpose for every person under the sun, whether or not we fully comprehend it or believe it. Though His plans may sometimes seem mysterious, rest assured they are always good because He is inherently good.

If you feel inclined to connect further, whether for prayer or to invite me or my team to speak to your group—whether in person or virtually via Zoom—anywhere in the world, please don't hesitate to reach out.

May these materials continue to serve as a blessing to you.

We can be reached:
    Kevin Winkler
    Pastor@thechurchalive.com

    www.thechurchalive.com
    www.Alivemedianetwork.tv

    Also, find us on Roku:
    Alive Media Network

Cover design by: Rachel Howarton. For custom media artwork, media commercials, and related material, please contact Rachel at pastor@thechurchalive.com.

Jesus Christ is Lord!

# REFERENCES

1. Dictionary.com. "Revelation." *Dictionary.com*. Accessed January 16, 2025. https://www.dictionary.com/browse/revelation.
2. Dictionary.com. "Parable." *Dictionary.com*. Accessed January 16, 2025. https://www.dictionary.com/browse/parable.
3. Meyer, Joyce. *Battlefield of the Mind: Winning the Battle in Your Mind*. New York: FaithWords, 1995, 63.

# ABOUT THE AUTHOR

Kevin Winkler's journey with his faith began at an early age, a calling that seemed almost predestined. As a child, Kevin would line up his stuffed animals and preach to them, playing church with unwavering sincerity. This early passion for preaching the Word of God was not a mere phase but a foreshadowing of his life's work.

Kevin is deeply committed to authenticity in his ministry. He fervently desires for others to experience an intimate friendship with Jesus and to see the Father in a deeper, more personal way. This drive for genuine connection and spiritual growth has been the cornerstone of his ministry.

With over 20 years of full-time ministry experience, Kevin Winkler is the founder of Church Alive in Waco, Texas, alongside his wife, Misty. Together, they also established the Alive Media Network, expanding their reach and impact within the community and beyond.

Kevin's ministry is not just about preaching; it's about fostering a sense of family and community within the church. He takes great joy in being with his "church" family, witnessing their victories in life, and supporting them through their journeys.

Kevin and Misty are blessed with a beautiful daughter, and they reside in Texas, where they continue to serve and inspire others through their faith and dedication.

To watch or participate in a broadcast by Kevin Winkler visit www. alivemedianetwork.tv or on a Roku device download Alive Media Network

If you would like Kevin Winkler to speak at your church or event please contact Kevin.

Email: pastor@thechurchalive.com